Daniel

Elizabeth Grech

Daniel

Acknowledgements

I would like to thank Stephen Matthews and Ginninderra Press for believing in my book and the importance of my story.

Gratitude and many thanks go to my extremely patient and hardworking editor, as well as my loving and supportive family, husband and daughter.

Last but not least my son Daniel, who has taught me the meaning of unconditional love and forgiveness.

Thank you.

Daniel
ISBN 978 1 76109 062 2
Copyright © Elizabeth Grech 2021

First published 2021 by
GINNINDERRA PRESS
PO Box 3461 Port Adelaide 5015
www.ginninderrapress.com.au

Dedication

For one and all

Prologue: February 2013

I waved goodbye to Daniel and watched as he walked with a teacher aide to his classroom. I felt nothing. I was aware that it was possibly the last time I would ever see my son, but I didn't feel anything.

I knew that eventually we would have to surrender Daniel. It was the first thing my parents told me when I had broken the news of Daniel's diagnosis to them. I just didn't expect to feel nothing when it happened.

It had been a bad morning. Every day was difficult and today hadn't been an exception. Daniel had been anxious all morning and, to cope with his anxiety, had repeated his mantras without pause. I had packed Daniel's respite bag with him last night. He wasn't happy that he was going to respite but, after crying and throwing tantrums, eventually accepted it. Daniel was completely oblivious to the fact that Thursday night would be his last night with us.

We were drained and emotionally depleted. Our life revolved around Daniel and consisted of his never-ending tantrums. We loved our son, but he impacted negatively on every aspect of our life and made it unbearable. The life we had was a far cry from the idyllic life we had envisioned thirteen years earlier.

One

Daniel was born at 12.14 a.m. on 1 June 2000. He was delivered by Caesarean, after it was realised that he was a brow presentation. I was in labour for approximately twelve hours before this. He was jaundiced, had swollen eyes and looked like he had just done several rounds with Mike Tyson. He was the most beautiful baby in the world, and I felt overwhelmed with love for this tiny, fragile, perfect creature.

He didn't cry as I expected but made small, kitten-like sounds. I soothed him as I gazed at his perfect face. He had all his limbs, ten fingers and ten toes; I didn't need him to holler like crazy – he was everything we had hoped for. We were relieved after all the worry and anxiety, caused by the discovery of extra fluid at the back of Daniel's neck, during my twelve-week ultrasound. We felt joy, responsibility and, more than anything, an overwhelming love for our perfect boy.

Before we left the hospital, Daniel was given a number of standard tests just to make sure everything was as it should be. All test results were normal, with the exception of his heart. A small hole was detected, and we were advised to take him to a cardiologist when he was six months old. The hole should have repaired itself by then. If it remained, then he would need treatment or possibly an operation. It did put a damper on things; it was hard to believe that he could possibly have anything wrong with him. It was all too easy to believe that our beautiful baby boy was healthy and perfect.

We left the hospital a couple of days after Daniel was born. He had been a perfect textbook baby, so I left feeling confident, relaxed and well rested. That rapidly changed once we got home.

We had been shown how to bath Daniel, so we gave him his first bath. After dressing him in a new baby romper, feeding and burping him, we put him to sleep in his new bassinet. He slept without any fuss or difficulty, and Simon and I wondered why so many parents are sleep-deprived.

Simon looked at me and stated, 'Well, that was too easy.'

'I know,' I agreed. 'Why are parents so tired all the time? This whole baby thing seems pretty easy.'

He slept for approximately three hours. It was the first and only time he slept in his bassinet. For the rest of the night, Simon and I took shifts holding Daniel. It was the only way we were going to get any sleep, as he screamed every time we put him in the bassinet. In the morning, we sought refuge with my parents, who lived six hours away. We stayed with them for a week.

After two weeks' holiday, Simon went back to work. Daniel started to settle and began sleeping through the night. Once he reached six weeks, we were able to get six hours uninterrupted sleep. I loved being a stay-at-home mum, and Daniel seemed to be thriving. The only concern we had at that stage was that he suffered constantly from constipation. We were advised by doctors to give him water that had been boiled. We were unsuccessful, as he refused to drink from a bottle. In spite of the constipation, he was feeding well, sleeping well and growing at a healthy rate.

When Daniel was three months old, I began to notice some behaviour which was unusual for a baby. There were times when he was completely unresponsive to me. Occasionally, he ignored me and just stared past me, as if he couldn't see or hear me. It didn't happen all the time, but it concerned me enough to mention it to Simon and my parents.

My parents were visiting when I first brought the subject up.

I casually asked my mother, 'Did I ever ignore you when I was a baby?'

'No, only when you were a teenager,' she laughed.

I explained my concern that sometimes, after a bath, Daniel acted as if he couldn't hear me. Both my parents reassured me with a barrage of explanations that he was fine.

'We all have times when we want to be left alone,' my mum said. 'You can't expect him to be responsive all the time.'

'He's probably just worn out after the bath, or maybe has water in his ears,' my dad added.

Simon agreed with my parents, so I let the matter drop. However, Simon and I tested his hearing just to be on the safe side. It was a primitive test that involved making a loud clap near Daniel. We tested both his left and right ear, and he looked at the person who clapped every time. We both agreed his hearing was fine and we didn't have anything to worry about.

Daniel continued to sleep and breastfeed well and was even enjoying jars of baby food. He was on track with his milestones, also being well within the healthy growth percentiles for a baby his age. He started smiling at six weeks and began to roll over at five months. We noticed that he wasn't a particularly smiley baby, and many people commented on this. He was also a relatively quiet baby and, although he wasn't silent, he didn't babble as much as other babies did.

At around six months, Daniel's first bottom teeth began to come through. Teething didn't seem to cause him much pain or discomfort, and he continued to sleep and breast feed well. Teething didn't cause the endless crying, screaming or temperatures that we had been warned about by parenting books and other parents. It did, however, cause him to stop eating solid food and revert to breast milk only. The struggle to get him to eat solid food lasted many years after he finished teething. Shortly after he turned six months, a cardiologist confirmed that his heart had healed itself. He advised that no further action or monitoring was required.

As Daniel was a quiet, well-behaved baby, I took him out every day. He loved going out and enjoyed the swings and slippery dip at the park. I chatted with other mums and was appreciative of the adult interaction. We mostly spoke about our children. We laughed at their crazy antics and commiserated about sleep deprivation, never-ending nappies and laundry. I laughed along with the other mums about the never-ending dirty nappies, though, at that stage, Daniel, was only doing a poo every second day. Constipation proved to be another ongoing issue that to date has not been solved. We didn't realise at the time how much worse the constipation would get, and how much of an impact it would have on all our lives.

Two

By the time he was six months old, I noticed that Daniel had developed some unusual behaviour. He was content to stare at things such as trees or clouds, for relatively long periods of time. While changing his nappy, I noticed he was more interested in watching the trees outside his window than interacting with me. He also smiled and sometimes laughed at inanimate objects or nothing at all. I mentioned this to my parents, as well as other mums at the park.

Once at the park, another mum noticed and commented, 'Your little one is so happy. I wonder what he's smiling at? I can't see anything but trees.'

'He smiles and laughs at nothing all the time,' I replied.

'Oh. He might be remembering something that happened earlier or perhaps he's just a really happy baby.' Her response was both positive and reassuring.

Daniel smiled and laughed at inanimate objects or nothing, but was unresponsive to people. He didn't smile or engage with people as most babies do but stared blank-faced when someone tried to make him smile or laugh. Most people usually responded by saying, 'Oh, my goodness, such a serious baby. He must be an old soul.'

Having a large family meant that there was never a shortage of willing babysitters. One weekend, Simon and I took advantage of our family's willingness to babysit and went to a movie. When we came home, my older, childless brother told me that Daniel had smiled and laughed at racks of clothes. Although I had told my family about Daniel's tendency to smile and laugh at nothing, I have a feeling that they had to see it to believe it. The incident sparked a conversation about ghosts, and how children, usually four and under, can see ghosts. The conversation split the family into believers and non-believers, with Simon and me both firm non-believers. If Daniel was seeing ghosts, he would continue to do so well past the age of four. To this day, he continues to smile or burst into laughter at nothing.

There were other incidents that would have rung alarm bells loudly and clearly, had Daniel not been our first baby. One such incident happened while I was shopping with him at a chemist. A lady smiled at him, and instead of smiling back or even ignoring her, He started crying. It was embarrassing, and I apologised to the lady before continuing to push his stroller around the chemist. It was the first time I felt embarrassed by his behaviour, but unfortunately it wasn't the last. I thought his reaction odd, and I overheard enough of the lady's phone conversation to realise that I wasn't the only one. It's never nice to hear people make negative comments about your baby, but it was something that would happen more frequently as he grew up.

When I was pregnant with Daniel, one of the things that Simon and I agreed on was that we wouldn't spoil him. We would only give toys for his birthday and for Christmas. By the time he was nine months old, we had four full boxes of toys. He had almost every toy made for a baby but very little interest in any of them.

At nine months, Daniel stood for the first time. A few days later, he began to walk, while holding onto the walls or furniture for support. The way he walked was very similar to someone learning to skate, using a wall for support. If there were any gaps between the furniture, he would slowly drop to the floor and then crawl to the next piece of furniture. He was also quite happy to walk while holding someone's hand. When he wanted to walk, all he needed to do was hold out his hand, and either Simon or I would go to him. Although he didn't even attempt to stand or walk independently, we assumed that it wouldn't be long before he would progress to doing this. At twelve months, he still wasn't any closer to walking or even standing unaided. We found this odd, given that he had been walking with support for three months. It didn't matter what we did, or how much encouragement we gave him, He refused even to try standing or walking by himself.

Daniel's reluctance to walk brought about the usual barrage of excuses. We blamed everything and everyone. My dad, who was an orthopaedic surgeon, checked his hips for any previously missed dislocations. His hips, as suspected, were fine, but my dad, keen to be certain said, 'It's good to be sure.'

As the months passed, Daniel's walking, or not walking, seemed to become an obsession for everyone and overshadowed other things that were just as important, if not more so. My parents and Simon's parents continued to ask if he was walking, and I continued to answer 'No' through gritted teeth. Unknown to me, my parents spoke to a paediatrician who lived in their area. Without seeing him, the paediatrician's advice was to take him to a doctor. It was good advice but, unfortunately, we didn't take it.

Daniel took his first independent steps at seventeen months, and it was a relief more than anything else. His reluctance to walk had become a source of tension for Simon and me. Once he started, he walked as if he had been doing so for months. We hoped that our concerns for his development were over, and that he would continue to learn and develop at the same rate as his peers. We were completely wrong, and he started to fall behind in both growth and development.

At eighteen months, Daniel was still only taking breast milk. I continued to try a variety of baby foods, as well as foods that most babies and children love, such as pumpkin, fruit and pasta. I even gave him chocolate, chips and biscuits, all of which he reluctantly nibbled. I tried letting him feed himself. He ate nothing and made a mess. The only foods that he took independently were apple juice and teething rusks. I was so desperate to get him to eat that I would break off tiny pieces of fruit sticks, roll them into little balls and then pop the balls into his mouth. I gave him at least two fruit sticks a day using this unconventional method. I tried this with other food but was unsuccessful. In spite of his reluctance to eat, he wasn't a thin or sickly baby and, although a little small for his age, still looked well fed. He was also very healthy.

Although the fruit sticks were high in fibre, Daniel continued to have constipation. He seemed to be in pain when going to the bathroom and was only soiling his nappy every other day. He was at the age where he should have been weaned, but I was reluctant to wean him as he wasn't eating. I was so focused on feeding him that I barely noticed that his language hadn't started to develop as it should.

Daniel said his first word at twelve months. He pointed to a light in the car and said very clearly, 'gay'. At eighteen months, he could still say only one word. Although he wasn't silent, he didn't babble nearly as much as other younger babies. He also didn't answer questions by nodding or shaking his head, like other toddlers did.

Worried that Daniel's speech wasn't developing, I started taking him to a playgroup every Wednesday for two hours. I also continued taking him to the park and shops every day. Simon and I played with him, sang and read to him constantly with the hope of encouraging and stimulating speech. His grandparents also did everything they could to coax him to speak. His reluctance to speak was met with both excuses and reassurances. The excuses were, as always, many and varied. Our favourite excuse was that boys take longer to speak than girls.

The ladies at Daniel's playgroup were friendly and incredibly supportive, as were most other mums that I encountered on my daily visits to the parks. Many would be taken aback by his lack of speech, but most were reassuring. I heard numerous stories about people's aunt/uncle/cousin/friend's baby who didn't speak until they were five. It seemed that almost everyone I met knew someone with a child who had been very slow to speak. Most mums, after telling me about the child who was slow to speak, would assure me that all children are different, and that he would speak when he was good and ready. Many a kind mother would smile and tell me that he would be speaking before too long, and I would be wishing he would shut up.

I didn't actually believe any of the stories about children not speaking until they were five and suspected that they were grossly exaggerated. I never voiced my disbelief and instead, readily and happily agreed. I found myself saying, 'All children are different', 'Children all learn at their own pace' and 'Boys are slower than girls' so often that they became my mantras. Of course, I didn't believe a word of them.

One thing Simon and I noticed about Daniel was that he had an incredible sense of direction. He would start kicking his legs with excitement as soon as we turned onto the street where his playgroup was held, even though the playgroup wasn't visible. He really loved playgroup, though he didn't actually play with any of the other children. He also loved parks and threw a tantrum if we walked past a playground and didn't stop and allow him to play. We had to change the way we walked to the shops, in order to avoid passing any parks. It wasn't enough just to avoid the park; because of his acute sense of direction, we had to avoid the street the park was on. We were bowing down to him, and we allowed ourselves to be dictated to by him.

My parents visited fairly regularly and were always happy to babysit Daniel, allowing Simon and me some much needed time to ourselves. As he was about twenty months and walking independently with confidence, his speech, or lack of it, became my parents' primary focus. Theys spent hours with him trying to get him to say simple words that most toddlers could say. It was all to no avail, until one day when my mum returned from their outing with him, triumphant. Daniel had said the word *blue*. We were all ecstatic, foolishly believing that he had learnt his second word. Unfortunately, he hadn't added a second word to his vocabulary; he had just replaced his first word *gay* with the word *blue*.

A pattern was established, with Daniel learning just one word, using it for a month or so and then replacing that word with another new word. He had a one-word vocabulary, and Simon and I affectionately referred to that word as 'word of the month'. Although he was behind with his speech and still not eating, his behaviour was still relatively good. We were able to continue going out with him. Life was simple. Life was good.

Unfortunately, as Daniel grew, the gap between his development and that of his peers also increased, to a point that it was almost impossible to deny that there was an issue. Being first-time parents, we were able to ignore the issue for over six months. His grandparents weren't able to and took to nagging us, with the same relentless vigour that they had used previously when he was slow to start walking. It seemed that every phone call always included the dreaded question, 'Has Daniel started talking?' The question wasn't appreciated and was answered through gritted teeth, sometimes accompanied by a fed-up sigh. In spite of reassurances that we would call and let them know when his speech had improved, all of his grandparents never failed to ask, 'Is Daniel talking?' With patience wearing thin, and tensions on the increase, Simon and I needed some good news. It came in the form of two faint lines.

The pregnancy was good news for everyone, except Daniel, who was still only taking breast milk and apple juice. Suddenly at the age of two years and two months, he was instantly weaned. I had my first and only ultrasound at twenty weeks. This time there weren't any concerns. The baby and I were fine. Unfortunately, he was still only saying one word a month, still suffered from constipation and continued to eat very little. He also wanted to be nursed and constantly put his hand down my shirt to play with the clip on my nursing bra. He continued to do this for many years after he was weaned.

Daniel's development had stalled. He was now well behind his peers. He didn't have any language – he didn't follow simple instructions such as 'Get your shoes', and he didn't interact with children his own age. As he was still severely constipated and didn't follow instructions, I didn't even attempt to toilet train him. He was also having problems falling asleep. Previously, I had always put him to sleep while breastfeeding him. He was staying up later and later, and we resorted to letting him fall asleep in front of his DVDs. It got to the stage where he wasn't falling asleep until the early hours of the morning. As his behaviour was becoming increasingly difficult, I was reluctant to wake him of a morning and let him sleep. This caused him to stay up later and later.

It got progressively worse and all too soon Daniel was staying up all night. After a night when he didn't fall asleep until eight a.m., I reluctantly agreed when Simon said, 'We can't go on like this. We have to start waking him every day at eight regardless of what time he sleeps. We have to be strict, and we can't let him nap at all during the day. It's going to be hard but we have to do it.'

It wasn't easy, and somehow he managed to get by on little food and six hours sleep a night. Gradually, his sleep improved, and he started going to bed between nine and ten in the evening. We remained vigilant, however, waking him at eight a.m. and not allowing him to nap during the day.

One thing that hadn't changed was that Daniel loved going out. He didn't like returning home and threw a tantrum whenever we did. His behaviour worsened, and his tantrums became more and more frequent. We continued to take him out, as his behaviour, although bad, was acceptable for a child his age. As he was small for his age, many people assumed that he was younger than he actually was. As his behaviour continued to get more difficult, we were more focused on dealing with his tantrums and keeping him in an acceptable sleep pattern, than his development.

'Do you think Daniel will be speaking when the new baby is born?' Simon casually asked one day.

I was surprised but not really fazed by the question. 'Of course he will,' I replied confidently. 'He'll be nearly three years old. If he's not speaking by then, something is seriously wrong. Don't worry, he will be speaking when the baby is born.'

In spite of the obvious differences between Daniel and other children his own age, I never contemplated that he could have anything seriously wrong with him. My ignorance might have been due to my own arrogance as much as his appearance. He didn't look disabled at all. Ignorance is bliss and, although I struggled with his behaviour, I was still genuinely happy. I loved him and loved having him as my son.

The remaining twenty weeks of the pregnancy flew by, and although I still spent all my time with Daniel encouraging him to speak, there wasn't any progress. I sang songs, read books, and played games such as peekaoo and ring-a-ring o' roses with him, but it was all to no avail. he still wasn't speaking.

I continued to take him to playgroup once a week and to the park every day. I encouraged Daniel to play with children his own age, but he never showed any interest in them. He also didn't know how to share toys and snatched them from other children. He started hitting children who took a toy from him or were reluctant to let him have a toy. I continued to supervise him closely whenever we were in public. I apologised constantly for his behaviour. Luckily, all the mums were very understanding and accepted my apologies.

At the park, I found the easiest way to deal with Daniel was to put him on a swing and push him. He loved the swing and was blissfully happy being pushed. All was well until another child wanted a turn on the swing. Whenever I had to take him off the swing, he threw an almighty tantrum. He kicked, scratched, screamed, hit and threw himself on the ground in an attempt to get his way. One thing Daniel never did, while throwing a tantrum, was say any words. This was one of the differences between his tantrums and other children's. The other differences were the intensity and frequency of his tantrums. Often they were so bad that the other mum would take their child on something else so Daniel could stay on the swing. It got to the stage that I was wishing other mums and their children would stay away from the swings so I could have some peace and quiet. Years later, experts would refer to this as transitioning, and Daniel would continue to have difficulty with transitioning for many years to come.

Shortly before Daniel turned three, I enrolled him at a local preschool. I had heard from other mums that there were waiting lists, and I didn't want him to miss out on a place. I was so keen for him to go to preschool that I even lied on the enrolment form. One of the questions was, 'Is your child toilet trained?' I answered 'Yes', telling myself that he would be toilet trained by the time he started preschool. It was, after all, more than a year away. Another question was 'Does your child have special needs?' In spite of the obvious differences between Daniel and his peers, I still answered 'No'. It was with both relief and happiness that I answered 'No,' and I was still so very grateful to have a child who wasn't disabled.

Three

Jessica was born at 6.15 a.m. on 2 May 2003 but, unlike Daniel, cried loudly as soon as she was born. Her birth changed us from a couple with a child to a family, and I felt that my family and life was perfect.

I had a short but blissful stay at the hospital, while Simon looked after Daniel at the unit. Simon and Daniel visited every day, as did all our family. My parents offered to look after Daniel for a night, and Simon gratefully accepted their help. The next morning, my parents told me about their night with Daniel. It seemed his insomnia wasn't restricted to our unit, and my parents struggled to get him to sleep. In the end, they put him to sleep between them in their bed. My mum repeatedly told him to sleep. This technique proved relatively ineffective, as it just amused him.

Although my parents looked worn out, Simon looked well rested and relaxed after just one child-free night. When I asked my mum if they had woken Daniel up at eight a.m., she laughed.

'No. He woke up at six.'

Jessica was a textbook baby and didn't cause me any problems. I had heard from many mothers that their second child was easy compared to their first, so I still wasn't inclined to believe that anything was wrong with Daniel. I had also heard numerous stories about firstborn babies, and how difficult they can be. In my mind, Daniel was just a typical first baby.

We decided to spend a few days at my parents' house after Jessica was born. The drive was relatively easy, and although Jessica slept the whole way, Daniel didn't sleep at all. In spite of not sleeping and being woken up at six a.m. that day, he still didn't want to sleep that night. We woke him at eight a.m. and, after failed attempts to feed him breakfast, decided to go out. My parents joined us, and we all headed to a neighbouring coastal town. It was there that we decided to go on a relaxing two-hour river cruise. My parents looked after Jessica, who slept contently for the entire two hours. Simon and I looked after Daniel. On six hours sleep and an empty stomach, he was full of energy. He didn't sit for even a minute and spent the entire two hours running, climbing, falling, crying and causing havoc. It was all we could do to stop him falling overboard, and we were both relieved and worn out when the cruise was over.

We only stayed for a few days at my parents' house, but it was still long enough to leave us all exhausted. Jessica was a breeze, but Daniel was a handful. He hardly slept, hardly ate, couldn't be left alone and threw tantrums constantly.

Daniel still wasn't speaking, and we blamed his tantrums on his lack of speech. My parents also blamed hunger, and my dad spent every waking minute trying to feed him. Mostly he was unsuccessful, but due to his incredible persistence, he did manage to feed him sometimes. It wasn't enough to improve Daniel's behaviour, but it was still something.

After a few days with my parents, they voiced their concerns.

My dad asked, 'How are you going to cope when you're back in Sydney? How are you going to manage by yourself when Simon's back at work? Daniel is a lovely boy, but he is such a handful.'

I dismissed their concerns and, keen to reassure them, said, 'Don't worry. It will be fine.'

By this stage, Simon and I were very concerned about our son, and we wondered if we were doing something wrong. We compared ourselves to other parents and wondered how they coped with three or more children and did it so easily. We assumed that we were to blame, and neither of us entertained the idea that it could be Daniel and not us.

At home, we settled into our normal routines. Jessica remained a perfect baby, sleeping and feeding well. A couple with a one-year-old daughter lived in the unit next to ours. They left a card and a small present in our letter box. We took Daniel and Jessica to their unit to say thank you, and show off our baby girl. Simon and I met their one-year-old daughter and were amazed at the difference in behaviour between Daniel and their little girl. In spite of the fact that she was only a year old, their little girl could follow instructions, was well behaved and could say more words than him.

We returned to our unit, put the children to sleep and settled down to watch some TV. Even though we lived in a small unit, we still used a baby monitor. We had the baby monitor on and heard our neighbour's voice on it. She was on their phone and our baby monitor had somehow picked up the call. We should have switched off the monitor straight away, but we didn't. We heard her small talk and then listened as she began speaking about Daniel. She described him as having 'real behavioural problems' and said the parents were to blame. We were fuming and switched off the monitor in disgust. Angry as I was with her, and much as I hated her hurtful remarks, I suspected that her opinion wasn't an isolated one. I was angry because I knew she was right. I also knew that we were in the wrong and shouldn't have violated her privacy that way.

On my parents' insistence, I made an appointment for Daniel with a paediatrician. The appointment was on 5 December and was about five months away. I was still hopeful that he would be speaking by then, and I would have to cancel his appointment. I believed this, in spite of the facts; Daniel's behaviour was becoming increasingly difficult, and his development had stopped. I still took him and Jessica out every day, and I still spent the majority of my day looking after him.

On 30 June, when Jessica was two months old, I took her to be immunised at the local medical centre. I casually mentioned to the doctor that Daniel wasn't speaking, and that he didn't play with other children. I asked her, 'Is it possible that he is autistic?'

She didn't answer my question one way or another, but simply said, 'You should take him to the local community health centre.'

Her reaction floored me, and I felt sick to the pit of my stomach. I had assumed that she would reassure me that Daniel was fine, or dismiss me. I had wanted her to laugh and tell me I was just being overanxious and wasting her time. The doctor didn't laugh, reassure me or dismiss me. She gave me the phone number and advised me to call as soon as possible. That was the first time I realised that there might be something wrong with Daniel. It was horrible.

I went home and made an appointment at the centre. I was given the earliest available appointment, which was 3 December. The receptionist explained what would happen at the appointment, and I was also told I would be called if an earlier appointment became available. I felt good that I had taken a positive step but also felt that this wasn't a problem that was going to be solved easily, if at all.

I continued going to the park every day and taking Daniel to playgroup every week. At the park, other mums suggested taking him to a doctor. I told them that I had made an appointment, and most seemed to think that the problem would be solved. I wondered why they had so much faith in doctors, and what they thought the doctor was going to do to fix Daniel.

At playgroup, the mums were incredibly supportive, but Daniel's behaviour was becoming too much for even the most patient of them.

One day, Daniel was throwing a tantrum, when a pregnant mum with two young daughters tried to help. She got down at his level and very patiently and calmly said, 'Daniel, Daniel, sweetheart, you need to use your words.'

He didn't even look at her and continued to throw himself on the ground. It was like he didn't hear or see her. She was one of the most patient mums I had ever met, but she was clearly exasperated by Daniel and his behaviour. I apologised and explained to her that he didn't have any words. She was lovely about it, but I stopped going to playgroup shortly after anyway. It was only two hours, but he spent the majority of that time throwing tantrums or trying to hit other children. He wasn't enjoying it any more, and neither was I. Our world had started to get smaller, and it continued to shrink for many long years.

I continued taking Daniel to the park and supervised him closely. I also persisted in trying to feed him and failed dismally more often than I succeeded.

One morning at the park, after rejecting my many offers of food, Daniel joined a group of people having a picnic. He just walked over, sat on the rug and started helping himself to the chips and other snacks that they had laid out on the blanket. I apologised to the surprised and amused group and took him on a swing.

Although he didn't like the company of children, Jessica included, he did like adults. It wasn't the first time he had decided to join complete strangers. On another occasion, while we were going for a walk on the beach, he decided to join a couple of elderly gentlemen fishing. The two men were sitting on beach chairs, and Daniel sat quietly on the spare beach chair that was between them. Much to the fishermen's amusement, he made himself right at home. He was definitely not shy and appeared fairly sociable, in spite of his lack of communication.

He was also fearless and needed to be watched closely at all times. One of his favourite things was strollers, both baby strollers and toy strollers. He loved pushing his own stroller and also loved sitting in toy strollers while other children pushed him. This was as close to playing with other children as Daniel got. Although the swing remained his favourite thing at the park, he was also very fond of the slippery dip. It was a relatively high one, so I always went on it with him.

One day, I decided to give Jessica a turn on the baby swing. I pushed her from behind, so I could keep a watchful eye on Daniel. He was playing by himself in the sandpit and seemed fine, so I began to relax and turned my attention to Jessica. I continued to check on Daniel. Playing in the sand involved mixing sand and twigs with a wooden spoon, in a plastic bowl. We had been at the park for a while, so I decided to take Jessica off the swing and put her back in her baby carrier. I looked over at the sandpit where Daniel was previously playing but I couldn't see him. My stomach dropped, and I rapidly scanned the park to see where he was. The park was fully fenced, so I felt confident that he couldn't have left the park. I didn't see him at all, until I looked up at the slippery dip.

The top of the slippery dip was becoming very crowded, with at least five children waiting at the top for their turn, and more children climbing up. Daniel was at the top. He was sitting happily in a toy stroller, just waiting for another child to give him a push. I bolted over, before one of the children, sick of waiting for their turn, decided to push him. Relieved, I took an unusually placid Daniel home.

After Daniel turned three, his behaviour worsened. He threw tantrums all day, every day. The tantrums were intense but short-lived. He cried, screamed, threw himself on the ground and kicked, scratched and hit anyone who came near him. Tantrums were over anything and everything – if his crayon or biscuit broke, if an ad came on TV, if a TV show finished, if he couldn't do something, or if we dropped or spilt anything on the floor. He threw a tantrum when I took him off a swing, left a park, went past a park without stopping, and any time we returned home. Frustrating as these tantrums were, the worst were the tantrums where we couldn't identify the cause, as we had no way of avoiding them.

Mostly we dealt with these tantrums by distracting him. It was difficult, and I lost my patience with him many times throughout the day. I shouted at Daniel, was rough with him, and I even smacked him. I never smacked him hard enough to physically hurt him, or leave marks, but I knew that I was hurting him. I hated myself for it, but I still couldn't stop myself from shouting at him and hitting him. No matter how hard I tried, I could not get through a single day with him without losing it at least once. I hated being with him. I wasn't tired, but the only thing I wanted to do was sleep. I looked forward to sleeping and hated waking up. After I would lose it with him, he would cry and look at me with fear in his eyes and tears running down his cheeks. He would break my heart, and I would be overwhelmed with guilt. I would comfort him, all the while knowing that I would more than likely be shouting at him and hitting him again before the day was over.

As well as using distraction to deal with tantrums, we also started avoiding things and situations that could potentially cause a tantrum. I stopped giving him icy poles, biscuits, pencils and crayons and threw away or hid toys that caused tantrums. Our days started to get longer as we struggled to pass the time, and our world continued to shrink.

Daniel also became sensitive to sounds and would be upset by any loud noises. He didn't like lawnmowers, hand dryers, vacuum cleaners, power tools, balloons and children screaming. We avoided these things and modified our behaviour as much as possible. I stopped vacuuming and used a carpet sweeper. It was ineffective, and our carpet changed from a beautiful cream colour to a disgusting cross between light brown and grey. It also became covered in stains and revolting to look at.

Daniel developed a fear of Billy Connolly and threw a tantrum anytime he was on TV. At the time, Billy Connolly used to endorse an insurance company. We avoided watching anything with him in it, and any program that was sponsored by that insurance company. If we were watching a program and the commercial for the insurance company played, we frantically changed channels. It didn't happen often, but occasionally the commercial would play on two different channels at exactly the same time. When we watched TV, we clutched a remote and stayed alert to avoid the ad. We also were extremely careful when we poured drinks or carried things and avoided other actions, like breaking a piece of chocolate from a block. We did everything we could to minimise Daniel's tantrums. It was exhausting and extremely frustrating, as, no matter what we did, he still threw tantrums.

Although Daniel didn't have a lot of interest in his toys, he was intrigued by ordinary household items. He particularly enjoyed lining up similar things. One morning, he took all the plates out of the kitchen cupboards and placed them in a perfectly straight line across the kitchen floor. He regularly lined up plates, pegs, coins and anything else that he could get his hands on. It occupied him and was one of the only activities that didn't end with a tantrum. As well as lining things up, Daniel also enjoyed stacking things. He particularly liked stacking cans of Coke and made many tall towers in the kitchen. The towers, however, would all too often collapse, and the activity would end in a tantrum. We were, at the time, completely unaware of how typical these repetitive behaviours are for autistic children.

Daniel enjoyed mixing things in a metal bowl with a wooden spoon. We gave him dry ingredients such as flour, breadcrumbs and icing sugar. He also added other non-edible items, such as pegs or tissues. We didn't give him any wet ingredients such as milk, and he didn't ever taste what he made. We referred to this as 'cooking' and he continued to enjoy 'cooking' for many years to come.

Meanwhile, Jessica was an angel and continued to feed and sleep well. As she continued to grow, the differences between her and Daniel became more and more obvious. Like Daniel, Jessica smiled at six weeks but, unlike him, she smiled easily and didn't need a lot of encouragement. Jessica also made constant eye contact with everyone and would actively seek out attention from people. She was a happy, easy-going baby, who only cried when she wanted to be fed, or when Daniel hit her. Daniel actively disliked Jessica and hit or pushed her at every opportunity.

As Daniel still wasn't speaking, I was eager to do anything I could to help him. From a very early age, he had shown a great love of music and dancing. The first time we realised his love of music was when he was nine months old. He had just been bathed and was sitting, slumped in front of the TV. The theme song to a new show started playing, and he instantly perked up. He sat up straight and started twisting his upper body, back and forth, in time to the music. It was a funny sort of dance, and he did it whenever he heard that music. For the duration of the theme tune, he was very happy. As he grew older, he danced to other themes from TV shows. Given his love of music, I thought music might be the best way to encourage him to speak. I decided to enrol him in a music appreciation class for mums and toddlers. The class ran for an hour a week, was affordable and was in walking distance from our unit. It sounded perfect. Even if it didn't help, it would entertain him and kill an hour, in what were very long days.

The class was for toddlers and mums, so Daniel, at just over three, was the oldest child by about a year. Unfortunately, he was still far behind the other children in speech, development and behaviour. He was the worst behaved child there and threw at least one tantrum a lesson. He didn't follow instructions, wouldn't share toys and ignored the music teacher. The music teacher may have suspected that he had special needs, as she was extremely patient with him. She was a lovely young musician and made the lessons as pleasant as possible. Unlike the playgroup we had previously attended, the other mums were less than friendly and looked down on me. I was judged as an incompetent, unfit mother, with a spoiled brat for a son.

One day, I had been shopping and arrived at the lesson with my shopping in plastic bags in the bottom of my pram. I had just taken my seat on the mat, when one of the boys started throwing a massive tantrum. He regularly threw tantrums, so I didn't pay any attention to him. His mum was less than impressed and just glared at me.

One of the other mums noticed and said, 'Oh, my goodness, Claire, Charlie is so upset. What happened?'

She rolled her eyes, and in a voice dripping with sarcasm replied, 'Chocolate, someone bought chocolate, and now Charlie wants chocolate.'

Apparently, her son loved chocolate and had spotted the chocolate in my shopping bags.

I had no idea that Charlie wasn't allowed chocolate and made matters worse when I said, 'Sorry, Claire, but would it help if I gave him a small amount, just one square? It might calm him down.'

Her reply was a curt, 'No. I don't give Charlie chocolate. It's bad for him.'

I apologised again, to no avail. I was public enemy number one that lesson, and it was a long, painfully slow lesson.

Four

When 3 December arrived, as Daniel still wasn't speaking and hadn't made any other progress, we had no choice but to go ahead with his assessment. We arrived at the community centre at ten a.m. nervous and wondering how he was going to behave. We were also anxious about what we would hear that day – whether we had done the right thing in bringing him there, and more importantly, would the morning bring the help and solutions we so desperately needed. We were shown to a room where we were introduced to a panel of people, including a paediatrician, child psychologist and clinical student. The assessment process was explained to us.

The assessment was broken into three parts and took approximately two to three hours. The first part was to obtain a detailed history of Daniel's development. The second part was to observe his behaviour and how he interacted with other people. The final part was to discuss his diagnosis, and what services were available to help him. The paediatrician asked about my pregnancy and our family histories. We were nothing if not thorough and told them about the first ultrasound, which showed excess fluid on Daniel's neck, the show, the brow presentation, and the length of my labour. We were also questioned about our family health history. There isn't any history of mental health issues or disability on either side of our family.

The paediatrician then asked about Daniel's early milestones, including when he smiled, rolled over, sat up, crawled, stood and started walking. We mentioned that he was slow to stand and walk independently. In spite of the fact that he stood and walked with support at nine months, he didn't take his first unaided steps until he was seventeen months old. Before that, his development was on track. The paediatrician also asked about any concerns we had about him as an infant. We talked about his tendency to ignore us at times, his serious nature, his poor eye contact and his tendency to stare at trees and other inanimate objects. We also mentioned his lack of interest in toys, his constipation, his reluctance to eat and his habit of smiling and laughing at nothing. Again, we were thorough and left nothing out.

The paediatrician asked us about our current concerns, and it was then that the floodgates broke. Simon and I spoke at length about Daniel's lack of speech, his constipation, his sleeping issues and his tantrums. We had been dealing with his difficult behaviour for over a year, but we hadn't ever discussed his behaviour with each other, or with anyone else. Suddenly, our frustrations were being aired, and we spoke rapidly and at times over the top of each other. We had bottled things up for more than a year, and now that the bottle had been opened, we didn't hold back.

To keep things moving, and because we had already gone over the allotted hour, the paediatrician suggested that we start the observation part of the assessment. It was a relief to have gotten so much off our chests, but it was also a relief to stop talking and just do nothing. Daniel was taken into another room with the child psychologist, who showed him various toys and generally tried to engage him. For the most part, he was fairly responsive to the psychologist. He was also unusually complacent, and didn't throw any of his trademark tantrums. He didn't, however, speak, make acceptable eye contact, or display any imaginative play. The observation hour passed all too quickly, and we were asked to come back in just over an hour. The doctors needed an hour to compare their notes and make their diagnosis.

We decided to go for lunch at the nearby shopping centre. We walked, as it was a nice day and the shopping centre was only ten minutes away. On the way, we passed the medical centre where my pregnancy with Daniel had been confirmed. At lunch, we didn't say much to each other, and even Daniel was unusually quiet and well behaved. We had lunch at our favourite burger place, but with so much on our minds, neither of us even tasted our burgers, much less enjoyed them. The hour passed in an agonisingly slow manner, and with full stomachs and whirring minds, we made our way back to the community health centre. We were extremely nervous and anxious – neither of us wanted to hear the diagnosis.

'You were right to be concerned,' were the first words out of the doctor's mouth.

My stomach dropped. I instantly felt sick, and I wanted the floor to open up and swallow me whole. The rest of what he said I heard through a fog, and I had difficulty focusing and concentrating on what he was saying. It felt like I had left my body, and I was watching this horrible event happen to someone else. I wasn't a real part of this, just a distant observer.

'We believe Daniel has autism, as well as a global developmental delay. Formal baseline testing of his abilities, using the Griffiths Mental Development Scales, has shown that he has a moderate developmental delay,' the doctor continued. 'The tests results also indicate that his motor and puzzle skills are in the one year eleven month to two years and three months category. His communication and personal social responsiveness are in the ten months to one year two months category.'

We didn't react at all, or even say anything in response. I couldn't speak, but I forced myself to nod, after seeing the doctors give each other concerned looks. We didn't know anything about autism at that stage and were unaware that it was a spectrum disorder. The doctor explained what autism is. Unfortunately, because of his age, he couldn't tell us where Daniel was on the spectrum, or if he would ever learn to speak. We listened quietly as he spoke about Centrelink payments, support groups and various behavioural therapy organisations that might be beneficial for him.

We sat, feeling numb and taking very little in. At one stage, the doctor assured us that it was unlikely that Jessica would also be autistic. I was stunned, as I hadn't even mentioned Jessica, or given any thought to the possibility that she could have anything wrong with her. She was different to Daniel in so many ways; I really hadn't any concerns about her.

The doctor went on to say that we would be assigned a social worker to assist us. It was at that moment that I felt my whole world had collapsed. A very clear image of a poor, dishevelled, uneducated mother with several snotty-nosed, dirty-faced children under the age of five came to mind. The woman was living off welfare in an abusive relationship, and her children all had different, unemployed fathers. In my mind, this was the type of person who needed help from a social worker. Suddenly, I had been placed in that category.

The doctor stopped talking and asked if we had any questions. The only questions that came to my mind were 'Why? Why did this happen to us?' They were unanswerable questions, and I am not sure if there was any answer that would have satisfied me. The questions remained unasked and unanswered but would continue to plague me, every waking minute of my life. Sleep was the only respite from these self-destructive, pointless questions.

I remained silent but Simon asked, 'What about speech therapy? Do you think it would help Daniel?'

No one answered at first, and both doctors looked at each other with concern. 'It's worth trying,' one of the doctors finally said.

Speech therapy wasn't mentioned before this, and the doctor's unenthusiastic response to the suggestion made me think that he either didn't have much faith in speech therapy, or thought it wouldn't help. Either way, it wasn't encouraging.

The doctor asked if we had a paediatrician. He said it was important that Daniel's development was monitored. I didn't understand how monitoring his development would help him but didn't ask. Instead, I told them that we had an appointment with a paediatrician on 5 December. I gave them the name of the paediatrician, and they assured me that we had made a good choice, as he was a very good doctor. I wanted to ask how he would be able to help Daniel but, not wanting to hear the answer, I didn't ask.

Many months ago, my dad had spoken to a doctor about autism. He hadn't mentioned that it was his grandson. The doctor's response was, 'Tell the parents to take their child home and love him. There isn't anything you can do for an autistic child.'

The meeting came to an end. The doctors had given us all the information they could and had answered our questions as honestly as possible. At this early stage, there really wasn't a lot that they could tell us about Daniel's condition, or what the future held for him. In hindsight, it was probably for the best, and not knowing was kinder on us. We signed the Centrelink forms and took the reading material. We were told the results of Daniel's assessment would be posted to us in the next few days, and a social worker and psychologist would be in contact. The doctors wished us all the best. We thanked them for their time and left.

Five

At home, Simon and I didn't say much, and we went about our chores as if nothing had happened. I felt numb and drained of all energy. I kept busy with the kids and avoided even thinking about Daniel's diagnosis. My life had changed, and I didn't want to think about it, or deal with it. My worst nightmare had become a harsh reality, and I knew that I would never wake up from this nightmare. It wasn't until I went to bed that I started to think about the diagnosis. I cried myself to sleep that night and continued to cry myself to sleep every night for over a year. Simon and I didn't discuss the diagnosis that night or any other night. We didn't talk about it and just tried to get on with our lives to the best of our abilities.

Nothing really changed on that day, but I considered it as the worst day of my life. I felt as if my life wasn't worth living, and I wished every night that I wouldn't wake up in the morning. I wished for death at night and was disappointed every morning. The only thing that changed that day was me. I became angry and bitter. I hated my life, and I hated the world and everyone in it. The only exceptions were Jessica and Simon. I hated myself, religious people, happy people, positive people and people who worked with disabled children. I despised Daniel and wished that he would either wake up as a normal child, or not wake up at all. I knew he wasn't to blame, and I knew he was still the same child whom I loved so dearly. It didn't stop me from both blaming him and harbouring resentment.

More than anyone else, I hated people with normal children. The more children they had, the more I hated them. There weren't any exceptions, and I became lonely and isolated, as well as angry and bitter. I would see parents at the park, with normal, well-behaved children and just wonder, 'Why? Why couldn't that be me? Why couldn't I have that good, easy life? Why them instead of me? Why did I end up with the disabled child?' It was pointless, self-destructive behaviour, but I couldn't stop the negative thoughts. It was an unwanted loop that played constantly in my mind. I stopped socialising with other mums and glared at those who had well-behaved children. I scowled at mums who seemed to enjoy their children's company, and I took enjoyment from seeing them lose patience with their kids. I also enjoyed watching children misbehaving and felt happy when a child, other than Daniel, threw a tantrum.

On Friday 5 December, we took Daniel to his appointment with the paediatrician, a lovely, experienced gentleman. As suspected, the diagnosis of autism was confirmed and the prognosis was not positive or encouraging.

'Do you think Daniel will eventually learn to speak?' I asked him.

He was reluctant to answer but finally said, 'If Daniel isn't speaking by five, then it is unlikely that he will ever speak.'

It was disheartening to hear, and the future looked bleak. He also warned us about the many over-priced programs that promised drastic improvements in children's behaviour and development but delivered few, if any, results. He did, however, mention two places that might be able to help Daniel. One was an early intervention centre called the Lizard Centre, and the other was a special school called Vern Barnett.

After Daniel was diagnosed, one of the hardest things to deal with was the gap between our expectations of doctors, and what they were actually able to do. We hoped they would diagnose the condition and then promptly and without fuss cure it. The reality was heartbreakingly different. Once he was diagnosed, there was very little that could be done to help Daniel, and we had to continue living with his condition. We needed and wanted a cure even though we knew there wasn't one. If there was to be any improvement in his behaviour, it was going to take time and hard work. We were already exhausted and didn't have the patience or energy to work with him.

We celebrated Christmas, as it was Jessica's first, but as our morale was very low, we opted to have a quiet Christmas at home. To avoid frustration for Daniel and minimise tantrums, I removed all the packaging from his toys. I also put good quality batteries in them, so they were ready to be played with. I had bought a variety of toys that were suitable for three- to five-year-old boys. Daniel showed no interest in them and only wanted Jessica's baby toys. We continued giving Daniel toys in this way on birthdays and Christmases. I don't know how much it helped, but I do know that he still threw tantrums every Christmas and birthday for many years.

One of the first things I did after Daniel's diagnosis was go and see the local preschool where I had enrolled him. I told them about his diagnosis and found to my surprise that they were incredibly warm and supportive. I signed some paperwork, and the preschool director organised extra funding for a special needs teacher. Daniel was accepted into the preschool and would start two days a week, in February 2004. I also arranged for him to begin going to a local child care centre two days a week. I would be getting some much needed time away from him and looked forward to spending some time with Jess.

The weeks after Daniel's diagnosis passed quickly, as we were kept busy trying to get the help we needed for him. As promised, both a social worker and psychologist contacted me. The social worker came to the unit and bombarded me with information. It was overwhelming and not at all helpful.

At one stage, she lost patience with my lack of enthusiasm. 'It's up to you how much you take on board,' she said.

I didn't feel like it was up to me at all. I felt if it was up to me, I wouldn't have a disabled child. I didn't say anything and just nodded feeling completely defeated.

Frustrated, the social worker then asked, 'Have you started taking Daniel to speech therapy?'

'No, I haven't, but I have been taking him to music appreciation classes and playgroup, and I spend a lot of time playing with him and reading to him,' I replied.

The social worker was unimpressed. 'That's not enough to help him speak. He needs speech therapy,' she said.

It turned out she was half right. The social worker gave me three things: information about respite services; a number to call for speech therapy; and a referral for a community playgroup for children with special needs. Unfortunately, all three turned out to be nothing but a massive waste of time.

We had Daniel's hearing tested on 1 December. Although the technicians were limited in the number of tests they were able to run, the results of his hearing assessment showed that he had adequate hearing for speech. Given this result, and the social worker's recommendation for speech therapy, I phoned to make an appointment for therapy. I was given an appointment for a speech assessment. This was held on Saturday 11 December at the same community centre where Daniel had been diagnosed. It took over two hours, and a lot of the questions were the same as we had answered previously. At the end of the assessment, we were told that we would be put on a six-month waiting list. We didn't point out that he would probably change over the next six months, making the information we provided incorrect. We said nothing and went home feeling very drained.

I wasn't prepared to wait six months and on Monday made an appointment for private speech therapy for the following Saturday. On Monday, I also started going through the mountain of paperwork I had accumulated, from both the social worker and the community centre. It was time-consuming and, at times, disheartening. There were several numbers for services that provided respite, and I started by trying to organise some respite for us. The social worker had emphasised how important it was, and it was the only thing that I agreed with.

The first number I called was for a service that provided respite for disabled people over the age of eighteen. I tried a different number and was horrified at the price. A third number proved to be a respite service for elderly people. I called various respite services, and I was put through to different departments or told that someone would call me back. At times, I was cut off and had to call back and start the whole process again. There were a number of respite services that never called me back. I was at the end of my tether when I finally got through to someone who said they could help. I was overcome with joy and eagerly made an appointment for an interview.

The lady from the respite service came to the unit, and I welcomed her warmly. We started the assessment, and I answered more or less the same questions that I was asked at the community centre. I was saying the information for a third time and patiently answered all the questions. I was hopeful that something positive would come out of this assessment.

It was a standard assessment that was used for all clients, regardless of age or disability. The worker referred to it as a 'blanket assessment' and it included a number of irrelevant questions such as, 'Is Daniel married? Has he ever been married? Does he currently have a partner? Does he have children?' et cetera. There were also questions about cognitive skills and included 'Can Daniel cook? Prepare a meal? Do housework? Sew? Can he drive a car?' At no stage did she skip any of the questions, regardless of how absurd they were. There were many other ridiculous questions that I have since forgotten, in spite of being asked them numerous times over the years.

It took about two and half hours, and I was completely depleted by the end of it. When the lady had all the information she needed, she thanked me for my time and told me that someone would call me back.

'When will we start getting respite?' I asked, before she left.

'Well, at the moment we have a two-year waiting list. It may be longer if other parents are deemed as requiring more urgent assistance. It just depends on each individual and their circumstances,' she replied.

This time, I did point out that Daniel would change over two years.

'That's fine. We can do another assessment in two years' time,' she said, completely unfazed.

I never heard back from that respite service again. Hopes dashed and frustrated by the lack of available help and services, I plodded on.

A few days after Daniel's diagnosis, a child psychologist came to the unit to try to help Simon and me deal with Daniel. She was a mature lady and did seem to genuinely want to help us. We told her the main issues were his fierce tantrums and finding things to occupy him. She started making suggestions for things we could do with him and ways of dealing with his tantrums. Unfortunately, we had already tried and been unsuccessful with all of her suggestions. She would come up with an idea, and Simon and I would rapidly shoot it down. It must have been very frustrating for her but, to her credit, she remained very patient and calm. Perhaps it was because we kept apologising every time we dismissed one of her suggestions. It could also have been because we looked so worn out and exhausted.

At one stage, I asked if she had any children of her own. It turned out that she was an only child and didn't have any children. It was just her, her husband and the cat. She obviously loved her cat as much as any parent loves a child and she would become very emotional any time she spoke about it.

'Owning a cat is very similar to having an autistic child,' she even claimed at one stage. 'My husband and I have to have cat-free time. We have to have cat-free areas in our house, so we can have cat-free time.'

As she was such a lovely lady, and perhaps because she was so emotional, it was difficult to contradict her. So Simon and I said nothing and just stared in disbelief.

We continued with a weekly one-hour session for about two months, before we decided to stop. Lovely as she was, we weren't getting anything out of it. We found talking about Daniel and his behaviour very draining, and we needed to conserve what little energy we had left.

The private speech therapy sessions cost $60 for thirty minutes. We were more curious than hopeful and had no idea what speech therapy was going to involve. We understood how speech therapy could help stroke survivors and people with speech impediments, such as lisps and stutters. We just didn't understand how speech therapy could help Daniel, given that he wasn't speaking at all, or even trying to.

The first session was booked for Saturday, 18 December. The speech therapist was located off a main road, on the second floor of a tall building. Simon and I got in the lift at the ground floor, and after confirming we needed the second floor, pressed the number two. The doors closed with Simon, Jessica, and me in the lift, while Daniel remained outside. When the lift stopped at the second floor, Simon got out and ran down the stairs to the ground floor. I stayed with Jessica in the lift, and we rode back down to the ground floor. Simon and I arrived at exactly the same time and, to our immense relief, found Daniel standing in the same spot. We got back in the lift, this time with Daniel.

After that incident, we were extremely careful anytime we caught a lift or a train with Daniel. We would use a technique we referred to as 'the sandwich technique'. It basically meant that Simon would go in the lift or train first, and I wouldn't get in until after Daniel got in. It was a technique that served us well, and the incident at the speech therapy building remained an isolated one.

The speech therapist was a lovely, slim and very smiley lady who greeted us warmly. Her appearance and demeanour were a stark contrast to ours. We were both exhausted and, after the incident with the lift, frazzled. She looked about twenty, and I suspected that she may have either just graduated, or was doing work placement as part of her degree. What she lacked in experience, she made up with energy and enthusiasm. She introduced herself and took us to a small but immaculate room.

We sat down and the speech therapist turned to Daniel and in the animated manner of a presenter on a children's TV show said, 'Hello, Daniel. I'm Angie.'

Daniel ignored her completely. Unperturbed, the speech therapist tried to engage him by showing him different toys and books. Daniel wasn't keen on most toys and played with each one for less than a minute before becoming bored with it and moving on to the next. She then showed him some toy cars.

When he showed interest in the cars, she said in a slower and more deliberate manner, 'Look, Daniel. I have a toy car. Would Daniel like a toy car? Can Daniel say car?'

In response, Daniel made some sort of strange, animal-like sound that didn't even resemble a word.

The speech therapist heard this strange sound and with a triumphant smile turned to us and exclaimed, 'He said car.'

Simon and I didn't share her joy and just stared blankly at her. We laughed about it later that night, and it became our running joke. At home, whenever Daniel spoke gibberish, Simon and I made up what he said. Sometimes, we would just say one word, and other times, we would say whole sentences.

The speech therapist then started suggesting different 'cause and effect toys' we should buy for Daniel. Not surprisingly, a lot of the toys she mentioned we had owned at some point and had since thrown out, as they had caused tantrums.

She then asked, 'Have you heard about the Vern Barnett School for autistic children?'

'Is that a special school?' I replied. 'I was hoping that we could avoid sending Daniel to a special school. I want him to go to a mainstream school. That's why we're trying speech therapy, so he can learn to speak and go to a regular school. I don't want him to go to a special school.'

A little surprised by my response, she said, 'It's not a special school. It's a school for autistic children. Not all of the children have an intellectual impairment. It's a lovely place. The children all learn and play and are really happy there. It's a great school.'

I don't think she had ever stepped foot in that school, or any other special school.

As Daniel was starting to become restless, she took his hand and placed it in a bowl of uncooked rice. He left his hand in for a couple of seconds before removing it. She put his hand in the bowl for a second time. While she was doing this, she said, 'This is something you should do when he is having a tantrum. The uncooked rice will have a calming effect.'

We didn't say anything and just nodded.

Daniel pulled his hand out again, so she took him over to the toys and continued to play with him. He became frustrated by one of the toys and started throwing a tantrum. She put his hand in the bowl of rice for a third time. This time Daniel pulled his hand out and threw the bowl of rice across the room. The floor that was already covered with disregarded toys was now also covered with uncooked rice.

Mercifully, the thirty minutes had passed, and we thanked the speech therapist for her time.

We continued to take Daniel to therapy every Saturday, and she continued her attempts to engage him, through play, books and songs. After the first session, she never tried the bowl of uncooked rice with him again. One session, the therapist suggested a home visit. Simon and I were agreeable, and the following Saturday, she came to our unit for the lesson. She was surprised to find that we were living in a two-bedroom unit. She was also surprised by how tidy, and, with the exception of the revolting carpet, how clean the unit was. To avoid Daniel breaking them, we had packed away all our ornaments. She didn't comment on the fact that the unit was completely void of anything fragile or breakable. It was here that she told us that she was going overseas. We decided to finish the speech therapy, as there hadn't been any progress at all.

As speech therapy and sessions with a child psychologist didn't provide the help we needed, I reluctantly started attending the playgroup for children with special needs. Unlike regular playgroups, this one was very depressing. The children threw tantrums instead of playing and seemed to be very discontent in their isolation. They ignored each other and the staff, who very patiently but unsuccessfully tried to engage the children in play. None of the other mums seemed happy to be there, and it was difficult to make small talk. It was hard to know what to say to one another, as we couldn't talk or laugh about the cute, adorable things our children did. The other mums and occasionally fathers who attended the playgroup all looked worn out and depressed and were often dishevelled in their appearance. It was as if they had given up completely on life and themselves. I knew that I didn't look any different.

At the playgroup, Daniel started a new routine that we couldn't shake no matter how hard we tried. He began what we referred to as 'border patrol'. It involved him finding a short walking route and continuing on that route until we left the playgroup. Trying to divert him to a more productive task would result in a tantrum. He threw himself on the ground and hit and kicked anyone who was near him. He also covered his ears while he screamed a terrible, high-pitched scream.

While at the playgroup, I overheard one of the other mums talking to a staff member about her eighteen-month-old.

'Did I tell you that Jessie has been having speech therapy?' she said.

'That's great,' the staff member replied. 'Jessie's going to get a lot out of speech therapy and you're going to see a big improvement in her speech and behaviour. It's going to help a lot.'

I was curious and asked, 'Where do you go for speech therapy?'

'I don't go anywhere, the speech therapist comes to my house,' she replied.

'Wow,' I said, 'that's so convenient, but it must be expensive.'

She seemed puzzled and said, 'No. It doesn't cost me anything. Don't you get speech therapy for Daniel?'

'No. I'm still on a waiting list,' I said. 'How long did you have to wait for speech therapy?'

'I didn't wait at all,' she replied. 'Jessie received speech therapy as soon as she was diagnosed.'

It was fuel to my anger and the final straw. Given the depressing nature of the playgroup, Daniel's border patrol, and the fact that he hadn't made any progress, I decided to stop going.

I vented my frustrations to Simon later that evening. I whinged, whined and complained.

Fed up with my carry on, Simon asked, 'Which mum do you mean?'

'Jessie's mum. You've met her,' I replied. 'She has older children from a previous marriage as well as Jessie. You met her and her husband when you came to the playgroup on your day off.'

It took him a few seconds to remember, but his reply silenced me. He calmly asked, 'Are you seriously talking about the lady in tracksuit pants who looks like she wants to kill herself?'

Unfortunately, Daniel's border patrol didn't finish once I stopped attending the playgroup. He now did it everywhere we went. It limited the playgrounds we could visit to those that were fully fenced. This reduced our playgrounds from more than six to two.

One day, I took Daniel to one of the two playgrounds with my parents.

When my dad saw him doing his border patrol, he was upset and asked, 'Does he always do this?'

'All the time,' I answered honestly. 'If I try to stop him, it's worse. He just throws a massive tantrum. He's a nightmare.' I didn't mince words.

My dad, as always came to his defence. 'No, he's a good boy. He's just frustrated because he can't tell you what he wants. Why do you keep bringing him to the park? Can't you take him to other places?'

Frustrated, tired, and not wanting to hear anything that even remotely resembled criticism, I sighed and asked, 'Where? He's a nightmare everywhere we go, and he's even worse at home.'

My dad, at a loss for answers, shook his head. 'I'm so sorry. You have such a big problem. I wish I could do something to help.'

It wasn't a practical solution, but I did take some comfort from knowing my dad understood how hard our life had become.

The days were becoming very long with Daniel, and I struggled to occupy him. I had stopped taking him to either playgroup, and our trips to the two parks were getting shorter and shorter. He didn't have any interest in his toys, and there weren't any children's shows on TV before three p.m. He threw tantrums constantly and was only quiet when watching *Play School* and *Sesame Street*. He watched both *Sesame Street* and *Play School* in the morning and afternoon. More often than not, I would find myself counting down the hours and then minutes, until three p.m., so he could watch *Play School*. Sometimes he would only watch for a few minutes. Those were the worst days.

We thought a little break might do us all some good so decided to spend a weekend at my parents' house. My parents were delighted to have us stay, and my dad in particular, showered Daniel with love and affection.

When we arrived, he exclaimed unabashedly, 'I'm so happy. I've missed Daniel so much. I love all my grandchildren, but I love him the most.' He then turned to Daniel and after kissing him repeatedly said, 'You are such a nice boy. I love you so much. I've missed you so much.'

Daniel didn't take a break from his border patrol, and the weekend wasn't enjoyable or relaxing for anyone. Anytime we were at my parents' house, he wanted to do a lap of the backyard and front garden. As the house was on a busy road, he had to be accompanied at all times. He never tired of this repetitive loop, in spite of the sweltering heat.

We tried to take over from my dad, but his reply was always the same. 'I'm happy. I love to spend time with my special boy.' My poor dad, patient as always, must have walked nearly a kilometre and lost a kilo in sweat.

The only thing worse than doing border patrol with Daniel was trying to get him to stop. My parents were relieved and exhausted when the weekend finally ended and we returned to Sydney.

As Daniel continued to eat and drink very little, constipation remained a serious problem. He was now only soiling a Pull-Up once or twice a week, and his stools had become very dry and firm. He also seemed to be more agitated than usual before his bowel movement and was in a great deal of pain while having a motion.

One day, he was struggling. He was red-faced and sweating from all the straining and pushing but was still unable to poo. He was also becoming increasingly agitated and began to pace around the living room. After about five long minutes of pacing and pushing, a small poo started to show through his Pull-Up. He had managed to push it out but couldn't push it all the way out. It was now stuck in his bottom, with only the tip protruding. After a few minutes of rubbing his back, while comforting and encouraging him, it became obvious that he wasn't able to poo by himself. I took him into the bathroom, removed his Pull-Up and with toilet paper wrapped around the poo began to gently pull.

Much to his relief, I was able to pull it out. Unfortunately, it wasn't an isolated incident and happened frequently enough that I was able to develop a foolproof technique for pulling out poos. The trick was to pull gently, to ensure that the poo didn't break. It needed to remain whole if he was going to be given any relief.

Our unit was clean and tidy but was very cramped. We decided to try to move into a house further away from the city. It was around this time, that Simon and I started toying with the idea of moving to a coastal town, north of Brisbane. Simon took the first step, and put his name down for a transfer at work. As employment was going to be an issue there, I started applying for retail jobs. I knew, due to the nature and conditions of retail, that it would be the one industry that always had job opportunities. I started working all day Saturday and Sunday while Simon looked after the children. To cope with them, Simon drove them to his parents' house. The children were good in the car, and it was the only time they got to play in a backyard.

Our second appointment with the paediatrician didn't prove any more fruitful than our first, and I began to wonder what the point of the appointments was. The paediatrician was sympathetic and supportive, but it was becoming clear that,, unfortunately, he couldn't do anything to help us. He suggested blood tests to check for fragile X syndrome and also to check Daniel's iron levels. Simon and I didn't see any point to the tests and didn't want to traumatise him for nothing. My parents took Daniel for the blood tests, and he tested negative for fragile X syndrome. The tests also showed that in spite of his poor diet, he wasn't lacking iron. The paediatrician also suggested trying a support group for parents. Neither of us was interested in mixing with other parents, listening to other people's problems, or speaking about Daniel's behavioural issues. We only wanted and needed solutions. Unfortunately, there didn't seem to be any.

Six

Daniel started preschool and daycare in February 2004. He was three years and eight months but still wasn't speaking. He was still throwing tantrums and was still wearing Pull-Ups. I dropped him off at nine a.m. and picked him up at three p.m. Like a lot of children, he wasn't happy to be dropped off at either preschool or daycare. He cried and clung to me whenever I dropped him off. He was, for the most part, happy when I picked him up, and staff assured me that he had stopped crying very shortly after I dropped him off.

At preschool, Daniel had a special needs teacher who had the patience of a saint. She was a lovely woman, and he took a real shine to her. He was so fond of her that he even learnt to say her name. As the other four special needs children at the school were not disabled but actually children from a non-English-speaking background, his special needs teacher was able to spend some much-needed one-on-one time with him. This helped him cope with preschool. Even with the additional support, he still had difficulty transitioning and threw tantrums while at preschool.

Without the same one-on-one care, Daniel did struggle a lot more at daycare. He threw countless tantrums and continually tried to hit the staff and children. Transitioning was the main issue, as he struggled to move from one activity to another. He was also still fearless and had become quite a climber. One day, he climbed into the sink of a toy kitchen set. Even though he was tiny, it was a tight fit and taking him out of the sink proved very difficult.

As Daniel had become so attached to his preschool special needs teacher, he started saying her name whenever he became frustrated or upset. He did this at home and, unfortunately, also at his daycare.

One afternoon, when I was picking him up from daycare, one of the staff approached me and said, 'There was an incident today involving Daniel and I'm concerned about his behaviour. He was very upset earlier and was shouting, Die! Die! Die!'

'Oh, that's Di, as in short for Dianne, Daniel's special needs teacher at his preschool,' I explained with relief. 'He says her name at home anytime he's upset. He's become very attached to her.'

With Daniel at daycare and preschool, I had time to spend with Jessica. She was a pleasure to be with, and I loved it when it was just the two of us. Everything about Jessica and raising her was easy and uncomplicated. She was developing well and was hitting all her milestones either ahead of time, or on time. Jessica stood independently at twelve months and started walking very shortly after standing. She also started speaking at twelve months.

Much as I loved spending time with Jessica, the time I spent with her exacerbated my simmering anger. It gave me a taste of how life would have been if Daniel had been born normal. It was the life I wanted, and I couldn't understand why it wasn't my life. I had him when I was twenty-nine – according to experts, the optimal age to have your first child.

It made me hate parents with normal children even more. Listening to other mothers complain about how difficult it was to look after their children, and hearing their petty grievances, infuriated me. I hated these women with a passion and wanted to tell them about all the things I had to deal with. I never did, though, and continued to bottle up my anger and hatred. It also made me resent Daniel, and his disability, more than ever.

Mother's Day was particularly difficult for me, as I really didn't see it as any cause for celebration. I despised the build-up to Mother's Day and was upset by the seemingly endless commercials and images showing happy mothers, with normal, well-behaved children. It was salt in my open wounds and an unnecessarily cruel reminder of what I didn't have.

Daniel continued to be a very finicky eater, and we did anything we could to get him to eat. He developed a taste for Thai food, so we ordered it at least once a fortnight. He also liked pasta bolognese, which was given to him regardless of the time of day. On many occasions, Daniel was fed spaghetti bolognese for breakfast, after more conventional breakfast foods were turned down. My parents still looked after Daniel whenever they visited, and my dad continued to follow him around with food, in an attempt to get him to eat.

Packing lunches and morning teas for preschool and daycare proved to be extremely challenging. I was limited in what I could pack, as I couldn't pack chips, biscuits, chocolate or anything with nuts. I tried fruit, carrot sticks, muffins, pikelets, crumpets, muesli bars, cheese and crackers and various sandwiches. Daniel's lunch box always came back full, sometimes, with more food than I packed. I asked staff, on numerous occasions, if he had shown any interest in other children's food. The answer was always the same: they would keep an eye on him and let me know. I asked staff, other parents, looked in magazines and even searched Google for lunch box ideas. It was all to no avail. No matter what food I packed, he didn't eat anything at school.

As Daniel's development was extremely slow, he continued to fall further and further behind his peers. We couldn't continue to deny that he would have to go to a special school and enrolled him at Vern Barnet. The school was able to accept children from four years of age, whereas other special schools couldn't accept children until they turned six. Suddenly previous arguments about whether Daniel would attend a private or public school seemed decidedly pointless. Life had decided for us. We were invited to attend an open day at Vern Barnett, where we could meet the staff and see first-hand how the school operated. We went along and were surprised by how happy, upbeat and young all the staff were. It made Simon and me feel even older and more worn-out.

We arrived at Vern Barnett and joined a small group of parents. We were given a guided tour and shown around the school and the classrooms. The classrooms were small but very tidy and organised. Each class would have approximately five to six students and would have a teacher and a teacher aide.

Students were accepted from four until twelve years of age. The school had a closed door policy, which meant that parents weren't allowed in the classroom during school time. If parents wanted to see their children during school, they could make an appointment for an hour to observe their children from another room. Simon and I had no intention of observing Daniel at school, but listened politely anyway. There would also be mandatory teacher/parent meetings which would give parents and teachers an opportunity to discuss the student's individual educational plan (IEP). It was also an opportunity to discuss any behavioural concerns and develop strategies to cope with these issues.

At the end of the tour, the parents were given an opportunity to ask questions. The first question asked was 'What happens to the children once they turn twelve?' The reply was that some children go on to mainstream, while others attend a local special school. The next question was about how many children go on to mainstream, and how many children attend a special school. The staff successfully avoided answering that question, in spite of the parent's persistence.

Another question was 'What happens to autistic children once they are adults and have left school?' Again, this question wasn't answered, and the staff started to look uncomfortable. Parents also asked about whether their children would ever be able to work, or live independently. These questions and any others concerning the future of the children at the school were also successfully avoided. Without answers, many parents, Simon and I included, assumed the worst. It didn't build much confidence or trust, and various parents looked disgruntled and angry.

Working on weekends made finding a house difficult. We persevered and eventually found a three-bedroom town house further away from the city. Shortly after we moved in, I received a phone call from a public speech therapist. The phone call came nine months after we had Daniel's speech assessment. Since his assessment, I had made numerous phone calls to the community health centre and had been repeatedly told that we were still on the waiting list. As it had been well and truly over the six-month waiting period, I had given up hope that Daniel would ever receive public speech therapy.

The therapist came for Daniel's first half-hour session in the morning. She was young and polite, and I was eager for her to be more successful than his previous speech therapist. I listened to everything that she told me, and at the end of the session, we booked a second lesson the following week. When the speech therapist came for the second session, she let me know that she would be going overseas, and this would be her last session with him. She assured me that a new speech therapist would replace her. I didn't hear anything from the community health centre and, once again, I made numerous calls enquiring about his speech therapy. In spite of my persistence, he didn't receive any more public speech therapy.

Despite attending both preschool and daycare, Daniel's development was slow, and his behaviour hadn't improved at all. Now that he was four, his behaviour was completely unacceptable, and we attracted unwanted attention, as well as stares, glares and snide remarks wherever we went. He was also bigger, stronger and harder to restrain.

From a very young age, Daniel was blessed with a full head of thick hair that grew rapidly and needed frequent cutting. He was extremely beautiful and was also blessed with incredibly long, black eyelashes. From birth, in spite of being dressed in blue, he was often mistaken for a girl. At the age of eighteen months, we dressed him in a T-shirt, with the caption 'Best little boy in the world', a pair of navy shorts, and brown sandals and took him for his first haircut. We went to a children's department store which also had hairdressers qualified to cut young children's hair. We settled him into the chair, and the young hairdresser asked, 'How old is your little girl?'

Daniel had his first haircut and, with his new short hair, continued to be mistaken for a baby girl. We took him to the store every couple of months for a haircut. He objected to the store and the haircuts and threw a tantrum every time. It got to the stage where we couldn't even pass the store without him throwing a tantrum. We persisted and, in spite of his objections, were always able to get him into the chair. Once in the chair, one of us would hold him still, while the other distracted him long enough for a very patient hairdresser to cut his hair. It was an ordeal for all involved, but I couldn't stand the idea of him having a home haircut, so we persisted.

Just before Daniel was due to start at Vern Barnett, I took him to the shop by myself. As always, he started throwing tantrums the minute he saw the store. I ignored all the unwanted attention and continued to push his double pram into the store, all the while trying to reassure him. Once inside, I approached a hairdresser and asked, 'Are you able to cut my son's hair?'

He took one look at Daniel, who was throwing a tantrum in his pram, and just shook his head. I pleaded with the hairdresser and tried to assure him that I would hold Daniel and keep him still.

The hairdresser shook his head again and said, 'It's too dangerous. I can't cut his hair while he's acting like that. Sorry, but it's not safe.'

I left the shop feeling defeated and took an exhausted Daniel home. Later that day, while he was watching *Play School*, I took a pair of scissors and snipped the hair around his left ear. I repeated this on his right side. I then trimmed the hair at the back of his head. I continued and snipped at his fringe. The more I cut, the worse I made it. I didn't cut him at all, but I completely butchered his hair, and he ended up with the worst home bowl haircut in history.

When Simon came home that night, he took one look at Daniel, shook his head and said, 'What has Mum done to you?'

Daniel was accepted to start at Vern Barnett in February 2005. The fees were $600 per term. We were grateful that he was accepted but still bitterly disappointed that he needed to go to a special school. The uniform was a pale blue polo shirt, with a small school emblem on it, plain navy shorts and closed-in black shoes. As I don't have a driver's licence, and Simon was working full-time, Daniel was driven to and from the school in a school-provided bus. It was extremely punctual and reliable, and I found myself now dreading three-thirty p.m.

Although at that stage Daniel didn't have an issue with clothing, I noticed that many other autistic children did. In particular, one of the boys on Daniel's bus hated wearing clothes and was often completely naked when I collected Daniel from the bus. It wasn't too long before he started objecting to various items of clothing and footwear.

Shortly after we moved, I left the manchester shop and started working in a shoe shop closer to home. I was employed to work weekends and Thursday nights. About six weeks later, Simon started a new job as a driver. His new job required him to work different hours and different shifts. He worked noon to eight p.m. and arrived home at nine p.m. He stopped eating dinner with us and chose to have wraps instead of whatever meal the children and I had eaten. Simon also stopped eating during the day, choosing to eat only once a day. It wasn't enough, and in a relatively short time, he dropped around twenty kilos. Within three months, his weight dropped from ninety kilos to seventy. In hindsight, it was the first stage of Simon's eating disorder that continues to this day. I still regret not insisting Simon eat more.

Simon's new job also meant that I couldn't work Thursday nights, and I was fired from the shoe store about a week after Simon started his new job. It did, however, give Simon and me some time together without Daniel. One morning, after Daniel had been picked up for school, Simon and I were in the kitchen planning our morning. We didn't have any meetings or appointments scheduled and were relieved to have a couple of hours to ourselves. As Simon wasn't due to start work until noon, he decided to make himself a cup of coffee. He grabbed a cup and somehow managed to smash it into the new fish tank. The glass shattered, water flooded the kitchen, and our two little goldfish lay gasping on the kitchen floor, amongst the broken glass. We had bought the tank about a month earlier, after being told by numerous professionals that fish tended to have a calming effect on autistic children.

We frantically rescued our fish, picked up the broken glass, mopped up the water and then headed to the shops to buy a new fish tank. Our fish survived and were returned to a new tank before Simon headed to work. The fish were an additional time-consuming chore for Simon but, unfortunately, didn't have any effect on Daniel. Daniel was unimpressed by the fish and completely ignored them. It wasn't the first or last time we had been unsuccessful in trying to improve his behaviour.

Daniel's school used a communication book as a way of passing permission slips and information between parents and teachers. It was extremely useful. For many parents, Simon and me included, it was the only way to know how their child had fared at school that day. I was also able to convey messages and concerns about Daniel through the communication book. It was how I learnt about his achievements, behaviour and many antics.

It turned out that Daniel was still fearless. There was a student at the school in one of the older classes who had a tendency to hit other students. Many of the students were justifiably scared of him. One day at school, Daniel ran up to him, pulled his hair and then ran as fast as he could. In spite of being small for his age, Daniel still wasn't scared to take on the much larger, older student. His teacher later confessed that many teachers at the school found it hard to contain their laughter.

We were desperate for Daniel to become more manageable and were willing to try almost anything to reduce his tantrums. In spite of his being finicky and hardly eating, we decided to cut sugar out of his diet. He didn't eat a lot of sugar, but many professionals who had worked with him firmly believed that sugar, preservatives and artificial colours caused behavioural problems in children. We didn't have anything to lose and thought that it might actually encourage him to eat more healthy food. We were also concerned about his teeth, as he refused to brush them or let Simon or I brush them. He would clam his mouth shut at the sight of a toothbrush and threw a tantrum if anyone persisted.

At Vern Barnett, part of the curriculum involved taking students to a local supermarket, where they were helped to buy items of their choice. It was an exercise aimed at improving the children's social skills and teaching valuable life skills. One of the students from another class had successfully participated in the shopping outing and returned to the school with his purchase of a chocolate bar. The child was about to open his chocolate, when Daniel grabbed it out of his hands and devoured the entire bar. The other student wasn't happy and had a major meltdown. I wrote an apology in the communication book and, just to play it safe, sent two chocolate bars in Daniel's communication book. We stopped denying him chocolate after that incident, as withholding sugar didn't have any effect on his behaviour or help him to eat more healthily.

In Daniel's first year at Vern Barnett, he was in a class of six boys. The six boys were either four or five years old, and three of them were called Daniel. We found it quite bizarre that half the boys in his class were called Daniel and joked about it.

'Every time the teacher says Daniel, half the class will look up,' Simon remarked.

'Imagine roll call,' I laughed. 'Daniel.' 'Daniel.' 'Daniel.'

We found it funny, but knew all too well that when the teacher said, 'Daniel', or any other name, no one would look up.

In Daniel's second and final year at Vern Barnett, he had a lovely young teacher, called Yass. We met her for the first time at a parent/teacher meeting, where we had the following conversation.

'I just wanted to let you know that Daniel is having a little trouble saying my name. He's been calling me Ass,' his teacher said seriously.

'I'm sorry,' I said, trying to keep a straight face.

She was lovely about it and said, 'It's OK, but the other boys in his class are calling me Ass too.'

'I'm so sorry,' I spluttered, 'We'll try to teach Daniel to say Yass.'

It was one of the only times I actually felt like laughing at Daniel's school. Usually I wanted to cry.

Unfortunately, in spite of the school's efforts to improve his behaviour in public, Daniel still threw tantrums whenever we took him out. Both Simon and I were embarrassed and fed up by the stares, rude comments and unwanted attention. We also hated the good Samaritans who would either try to help and make things worse, or be sympathetic and attempt to empathise with us. On many occasions, while he was throwing a tantrum, somebody would tell me about someone they knew who also had behavioural problems. It was difficult enough to deal with Daniel while he was having a tantrum. It was even harder while trying to feign interest and, at the same time, listen to stories about difficult children.

We were also the recipients of a lot of unwanted advice. Some of it was practical, while much of it was ridiculous. Again, we usually heard the advice while we were in the midst of dealing with a highly agitated, screaming Daniel. Everyone who offered advice swore that their method worked and that it had improved their child's behaviour. The advice didn't ever come from parents of autistic children. It was usually from aunts, uncles, cousins, family friends and sometimes even neighbours of autistic children. We did listen to some advice and even tried some methods that other people suggested but, unfortunately, nothing helped.

We couldn't deal with Daniel's tantrums in public any more. We didn't have the patience to deal with other people and didn't trust ourselves not to get into an argument. We stopped taking him out and started taking it in turns to go out. We stopped going out as a family. We also began attending family celebrations either separately, or not at all.

The only time Daniel left the house was to go to school. He still loved going out and hated staying at home. Finding things to occupy him at home was difficult, and weekends, public holidays and school holidays dragged by painfully slowly. We stopped enjoying weekends and would count down the hours until Monday morning. It was a difficult time for everyone.

Boredom was the biggest problem, and Daniel sought out and found his own stimulation. At school, he enjoyed finger-painting. He liked the sensation of the cool paint on his hands and loved squishing the paint through his fingers. It was a sensory thing, and apparently he was someone who would actively seek sensory experiences. We tried, on many occasions, to let him paint at home but, unfortunately, it just made a mess and caused tantrums. It didn't seem worth it, so we stopped trying.

One day, I was at home looking after Daniel while Simon was out with Jessica. I put a video on for him and left him to watch while I got on with some housework. After about an hour, I suspected that the video was either finished or very close to finishing. Daniel was quiet, so I went to check on him and make sure he was still awake. In order to keep him in some sort of acceptable sleeping routine, we couldn't let him nap during the day. We had to remain vigilant, as we didn't want him to return to his nocturnal sleeping habits.

I went into the living room and, as I had suspected, the video had finished. Daniel, however, wasn't asleep. He was wide awake, standing in front of the couch in just a T-shirt. He was very happy with himself and turned to give me a big smile. He had done a poo and was now quite content in smearing it all over the couch and his face. The smell in the room was disgusting. He still suffered from constipation, so his faeces were particularly foul-smelling. I bathed him and then set about trying to clean the couch. The couch continued to stink for many months, and eventually we were forced to throw it out. It was the first but not the last couch that Daniel ruined.

Unfortunately, this wasn't an isolated incident, and Daniel seemed to take great enjoyment from smearing his faeces on his own body, as well as the walls and furniture. We did a lot of cleaning, used a lot of disinfectant and spoke to various therapists about it. They were able to explain the reasons behind his behaviour but didn't have any suggestions as to how we could put an end to his 'poo painting'.

Although Daniel was happy at his school, his behaviour and speech weren't improving. He still had very little speech and what speech he had, was used more for his own entertainment than actual communication. One of his favourite things to say was 'Grow up. Grow up. Grow up.' He said this constantly to Simon and me, as well as himself, and it never failed to make him laugh hysterically.

With the paediatrician's words still resonating and Daniel's fifth birthday only weeks away, I was resigned to the fact that he would probably never speak. It was a devastating realisation, and I didn't hold any hope for the future. I had accepted the fact that he would never work or live independently. I had given up on Daniel.

One day, shortly after his fifth birthday, Daniel was being particularly difficult. As he was irritable, I thought one of his videos would calm him down and possibly keep him entertained. I put a video on for him, and to make it start sooner, I cued the start of it to get to the actual program. He was intrigued by the video being played in double speed and wanted to watch the whole video that way. After that, he wanted to watch every video in double speed. My own impatience resulted in another activity being canned, and I cursed my stupidity.

We plodded on. We continued to take turns to go out and only very occasionally tried to go out as a family. Outings were limited to parks and drives, and they were exhausting and stressful. We had given up on ever getting respite and were resigned to the fact that our life was going to continue to be very difficult. Every day was a long struggle, and neither of us held out any hope that things would ever change.

It was around this time that we started seriously considering moving to a small coastal town in Queensland. There wasn't a lot to keep us in Sydney. The children still didn't have a backyard to play in; we couldn't go anywhere as a family, and driving and parking in Sydney was a nightmare. Daniel wasn't making any progress at his school; we weren't getting any respite; we didn't have friends; and I didn't even have a job any more. The only thing we had was Simon's job.

We were well aware of the employment issue and were justifiably concerned about money. As a way of keeping our costs down, Simon said he was going to drink water instead of Coke. It was the catapult that took Simon's eating disorder to the next level.

Our families didn't want us to leave, and my dad in particular was heartbroken. Although he loves all his children and grandchildren, he had developed a special bond with Daniel. Unlike everyone else, my dad didn't harbour any resentment towards Daniel because of his disability. My dad loves him unconditionally, has endless patience with him and isn't embarrassed by him or his behaviour. Although Daniel wore him out, he genuinely loved spending time with him, and there wasn't anything that my dad wouldn't do for him. Dad always found excuses for Daniel's behaviour and didn't say anything about him that wasn't positive. To my dad, Daniel was still his perfect grandson. The fact that he had autism didn't change anything.

Seven

We sold the townhouse and secured a rental in what would become our home town for the next ten years. We arrived on Friday, and on Monday, Simon secured full-time employment.

We took Daniel to the local special school to enrol him. We were met by the principal, a lovely experienced gentleman, who took the time to personally show us around and tell us about the school. He explained that Daniel would be in a class of five or six students and would be taught by both a teacher and teacher aide. As there wasn't any way that he could attend a mainstream school, Simon was anxious that Daniel was accepted at this school. He started explaining Daniel's behaviour and after letting him ramble for a few minutes, the principal calmly held up a hand to stop him.

'It's OK,' he assured us. 'Most of our students are autistic. We are well-equipped to deal with Daniel.' He also explained that many of the other students, including several Down's syndrome students, although not diagnosed with autism, displayed behaviour typically associated with autism. He then bent down in front of Daniel and tied his untied shoelaces. 'There is no doubt in my mind that this is the right school for Daniel,' he added, to put Simon's mind at ease.

From that day, the principal had a special bond with our son and often looked after Daniel when he became too much for his teachers. When he retired several years later, he was sorely missed by everyone.

The school didn't have a uniform, but students were required to wear closed-in shoes, if possible. At this stage, Daniel didn't object to wearing shoes, so we were not at all fussed by this requirement. The school also had a polo shirt which wasn't compulsory and was only worn by a few students.

We also applied for transport for Daniel. We advised the principal that as I didn't have a driver's licence, and Simon was working full-time, we would need transport for Daniel. Apparently, working was not considered a valid reason for being unable to drive your child to and from school. We explained to the principal that Daniel would have a tantrum when he was dropped off at preschool and daycare but was happy to be picked up by the school bus for his last school. It seemed to do the trick, and the principal told us to leave it with him, and he would organise the transport for us. We thanked him for his time and his help.

'That taxi service is the bane of my existence,' he added as the conversation ended.

We didn't understand the comment at the time but would understand it and agree with it, not long after.

After enrolling Daniel at school, our next priority was to try to find a paediatrician. We checked with his school, and although there was a clinic held there, the paediatrician wasn't taking any new patients. We saw a local GP and explained Daniel's behavioural issues, as well as the severity of his constipation. She gave us a referral for a paediatrician at the local hospital and was kind enough to write that Daniel needed to be seen urgently on the referral. As he had previously been diagnosed, we were warned that the waiting period could be up to a year.

With Simon working full-time and Daniel at school, it was just Jessica and me left at home. We made the most of our time together. We discovered a shop that was every little girl's dream come true and frequented it at least once a week. The owner was a lovely lady, and we fast became firm friends. I learnt that her son was the same age as Daniel and in the same class. It was a bizarre coincidence, and while I wouldn't wish a disabled child on anyone, I did take comfort from her friendship. She was honest, down to earth and, for the first time in a long time, I was able to confide in someone without fear of judgement. She shared my anger, frustration and resentment, and like me couldn't understand how, or why, we had to have disabled children. One thing we both noticed about our sons was that, in spite of having limited communication, both boys had an excellent sense of humour. The shop and the owner were a godsend for both Jessica and me. The owner was a true friend, and I needed and valued her support and friendship.

While Jessica was at daycare, one of the first things I did was look into respite. Although we could take Daniel to more places now, going out was still stressful. He enjoyed going out. However, he still threw tantrums which left Simon and me feeling worn-out. Daniel was still scared of many everyday things. These tantrum-causing things were everywhere. We tried taking him to beaches and parks that weren't popular, but we couldn't avoid all the things that Daniel was scared of. He was scared of balloons, crying babies and any loud machinery, such as lawnmowers, leaf blowers, planes, loud trucks, cars and motorbikes.

To help overcome his fear of balloons, we gave him ones that hadn't been inflated. Eventually, he overcame his fear of balloons enough that he was able to play with them. He became fascinated by balloon artists and would watch endless videos of people twisting balloons into various animal shapes. He soon began to imitate these artists and, using a balloon pump to inflate the balloons, twisted them into shapes that resembled grapes. He was fine with balloons as long as he was holding them. He was petrified if someone else had the balloon or he wasn't able to hold it. Simon and I firmly believed that it was a control issue, and that he had to have control of the balloon.

Daniel was also extremely scared of dogs and refused even to walk past a dog. He was scared stiff of all dogs, regardless of the dog's age, size or nature. His fear may have stemmed from an incident that happened when he was about twenty months old. While at a park, he was knocked to the ground by an overzealous Jack Russell. He wasn't hurt at all, as the dog was small and only playing. I picked Daniel up and comforted him. He wasn't upset for long, so I wasn't fussed by the incident. The owner was very apologetic and held his dog in his arms, so Daniel could pat it. As we lived in an area that had a high density of units, we very seldom encountered dogs. I was completely unaware that Daniel was scared of dogs until we lived in Queensland.

Daniel's behaviour was still extremely difficult at home, and Simon and I desperately needed time away from him. I contacted a number of respite services and found one that was suitable. A representative from the service came to the house, and we went through the registration process. It was a process that I was very familiar with by now, and I answered all of the behavioural questions as honestly and thoroughly as possible. At the end of the process, I was told that we would be put on a waiting list. The good news was that we were the only people on the list, so the wait wouldn't be long.

The service offered a variety of types of respite. It offered in-house respite, short-term respite, community outings, and a holiday program. We would be entitled to regular respite of three hours a week, where a support worker would look after Daniel at our house. We would also be entitled to short-term respite. We were never told on what basis our entitlements were calculated, and it never occurred to me to ask. I was just grateful that we would be getting any respite. Short-term respite would involve Daniel staying at one of the respite houses, for either a weekend, or from four on Monday afternoon till nine on Friday morning. The house would be staffed at all times by a support worker or, if needed, two support workers. All meals, bedding and entertainment would be provided, and all we needed to do was pack clothing and toiletries. Staff worked on a casual basis and couldn't work for longer than twelve hours. It sounded wonderful, and I was excited to start having respite. Simon and I were aware that it was only a band-aid solution, but it was the only one we had.

As school holidays were extremely difficult for us, I was also very excited about the holiday programs. Boredom was still a major issue during weekends and holidays. There were very few activities that Daniel could do that didn't end in tantrums. We were also still very limited in the places we could take him. The weekends, and in particular school holidays, were very long, and we struggled to find things to occupy him. I put his name down for the holiday program, explaining our dilemma to the representative. The program included things like fishing, barbecues, beach days and art and crafts. They were all things that I felt Daniel would be able to cope with and even enjoy. The program usually finished with an outing to the cinema. This was the one activity that I didn't include for him, as I didn't think he could cope with watching a movie at that stage.

I enrolled in a certificate three education course and, as part of the requirements, did my voluntary work placement at a local primary school. The staff were incredibly lovely and supportive, and I loved working as a teacher aide. I elected not to work in the special education unit at the school, as I desperately needed to have time away from disabled children. Unfortunately, unbeknown to me, working with disabled children was the only way to get regular work as a teacher aide. The work didn't diminish my anger, but rather blanket it with happiness and positive energy. The anger was still there, it was just buried under more positive emotions.

Things were still difficult at home. Daniel's behaviour hadn't improved, and Simon's patience and energy levels were depleting rapidly. As we were surviving on only Simon's income, he worried about money. Bills, in particular, caused a lot of anxiety and stress. He struggled with work and forced himself to exist on an inadequate diet of one insubstantial meal a day. His diet consisted of one meal of two wraps made out of Lebanese bread with tuna, lettuce, cucumber, tomato, Spanish onion and mushroom. Simon only used low-fat tuna and refused to put any butter, cheese or mayonnaise on the wraps. He also ate one piece of plain Lebanese bread, a cup of low-fat soup, six sugar-free lollies, two apples and a banana.

He was extremely regimented in his diet, and his daily food allowance was always eaten at the same time, and in the same exact order. He didn't drink juice, Coke or any other soft drinks and even restricted his fruit intake. He drank copious amounts of coffee in an attempt to ward off hunger and started having problems sleeping. He continued to lose weight and had become underweight. He is one hundred and seventy centimetres but only weighed sixty kilos. He refused to admit that he had a problem.

He continued to cook for me and the children, and cooked all the week's meals during the weekend. He refused to ever deviate from his diet and wouldn't even taste the amazing food he cooked. We didn't eat together as a family, and Simon and I ate at different times. He also insisted on cleaning up after cooking, as the way I cleaned up was not to his standard. He continued to push himself and to strive for perfection.

In November, we bought a modern four-bedroom house, approximately three hundred metres from our rental accommodation. After we moved to the new house, I started to understand the principal's negative attitude about Daniel's taxi service. I called the taxi service to advise that we had moved to a new address, thinking I would be able to update the address over the phone. I was told that we would need to reapply for transport, and that it would take up to three weeks for the new application to be approved. Luckily, Daniel liked walking, and for the next three weeks, I walked him to and from our previous home, where he continued to be picked up of a morning and dropped off of an afternoon. Even after our application for transport was approved, the taxi service occasionally attempted to drop him off at our previous address.

After we moved into the new house, Simon continued to put himself under pressure and pushed himself to get the new house up to his standards. He worked in a frenzied manner and was in a constant state of agitation. He began making to-do lists that were never ending and a constant source of pressure and stress for him. He repainted rooms, patched holes in walls, made repairs and continued cooking, cleaning and keeping the house immaculate. He did all this while working full-time, barely sleeping and eating an unvaried, insufficient diet.

He also started to weigh himself every day. He weighed himself in underwear, at exactly the same time every day. His weight fluctuated very slightly but stayed within a one-kilo range. Any weight gain, regardless of how small, caused him anxiety that lasted all day. Any weight loss made him happy. His happiness was very short-lived and lasted about five minutes. The weight continued to fall off Simon and his weight dropped to fifty-three kilos. He looked like a prisoner of war but he relished his slim physique.

Shortly after we moved into our new house, my parents came to visit us. It was roughly a ten-hour drive that my parents did over two days. The drive exhausted them and caused my dad to have terrible back pain. Nothing could keep him from Daniel, and they continued to visit every couple of months for the next ten years. My parents continued to babysit, and my dad was relentless in his efforts to feed Daniel. He also took it upon himself to toilet train him. His persistence paid off, and at the age of seven, Daniel starting using the toilet to wee. He didn't learn the skills of aim or control, so cleaning the toilets became a daily chore. It was just one of many little inconveniences that his condition caused. There were many others that impacted our lives daily and wore us down. We were always under pressure to remember to do certain things to avoid him destroying everything.

We had to hide all the scissors in the house, as Daniel would use any he found to give Jessica's dolls very short haircuts. We also had to hide all the markers, pencils and pens in the house, so he couldn't draw on the walls, Jessica's dolls, or anything else. It was frustrating that we couldn't find a pen quickly when we needed one. We all tried to be diligent in returning the scissors and markers et cetera to their hiding spots but, inevitably, we occasionally didn't. I cleaned many a wall, and a few of Jessica's dolls wore crew cuts and garish make-up that couldn't be removed. Simon painted walls regularly, and many quilt covers were ruined, in spite of my scrubbing and washing.

At one stage, Daniel learnt how to open a ring-pull can. He would go into our pantry and open any can that had a ring-pull. To avoid wasting food, we stopped buying cans with a ring-pull and only bought those that needed a can opener. It made shopping just that little bit less convenient and added to our frustration.

Daniel was bathed or showered daily, and it was a time-consuming chore. He often stayed in the bath for about half an hour, as he enjoyed baths. He wasn't quiet in the bath, but it did occupy him. Before his bath or shower, I had to remove all the bottles of shampoo, conditioner and body wash. If I left any bottles in the shower or bath, he would waste the entire contents of the bottle. I kept an empty bath wash bottle that I gave to him in the bath. Before his bath or shower, I would transfer a small amount of bath wash to this bottle. It was a baby bath wash to avoid him stinging his eyes.

I also removed all the towels from the bathroom and only left a bathmat and small face washer. Daniel used the face washer to dry his eyes when water splashed in them. If I left the towels in the bathroom, he would pull the towels in the bath with him. He splashed water in his eyes and all over the bathroom. When he wanted to hop out of the bath, he said, 'Hop out' repeatedly until Simon or I helped him out of the bath and into a dry towel.

After the bath, I would mop, clean the bath, put the soaked bathmat for washing and return the towels and toiletries to the bathroom. I tidied up and cleaned after Daniel constantly. It wasn't just the extra work and washing that frustrated me. It was also the relentless nature of his condition and the unfairness of it all. There were many other ways that we adapted, but as these ways became second nature, I have since forgotten them.

With Daniel's progress, it was often a matter of one step forward, two steps back. Sometimes, it was just two steps back. As he was partially toilet trained, we didn't want to undo my dad's hard work by keeping him in Pull-Ups. Unfortunately, although he was happy to stop wearing Pull-Ups, he refused to wear underwear. With Daniel out of Pull-Ups, bed wetting, regrettably, was inevitable. This stemmed from his chronic constipation. Every night, we took him to the bathroom before he slept, but if he needed to poo, he refused to wee. Even with a water-proof mattress protector, his mattress soon became stained and smelled of urine. The stench of his mattress overpowered his whole room and soon spread to the rest of the house. We eventually replaced his bed, and resorted to using numerous layers of waterproof mattress protectors, padded protectors and underblankets to protect the new mattress. In spite of all this, his mattress still needed replacing frequently.

Keeping the house, and in particular Daniel's room, smelling fresh was another ongoing battle. We couldn't use room deodorants, as Daniel is sensitive to various scents. The deodorants left him sneezing and caused him to have puffy eyes and a runny nose. We tried opening windows but, with his heightened sensitivity to everyday sounds, the windows didn't stay open for long.

Daniel was irritated by a number of common sounds, including lawnmowers, cars, power tools and, in particular, barking dogs. He hated when dogs barked, and he made a strange, donkey-like sound every time he heard them. He repeated the sound, becoming louder and more agitated, until we yelled at him to be quiet. The only way to stop the situation escalating was to shout at him. Even though our immediate neighbours didn't have dogs, we could still hear dogs from other houses on our street. Anytime someone went for a walk, it invariably set off a whole chorus of dogs. Even with all the windows closed, we could still hear the dogs barking. To try to help him cope with all the barking, we told him that the dogs were just saying hello. Knowing how much he loved music, we made up a simple song about the dogs. It was all to no avail, and the dogs continued to cause grief for all of us.

Another issue that started after Daniel stopped wearing Pull-Ups was the dreaded 'poo marbles'. Although he could control his bowel movements, he couldn't control the tiny specks of poo that fell continually from his shorts. These specks were roughly the size and texture of a sultana and littered our floors and carpets. Simon and I referred to them as poo marbles and we were constantly picking them up. It was another ongoing, losing battle that lasted well after Daniel was fully toilet trained. Unlike the poo painting that finished once he was fully trained, the poo marbles didn't stop until many years later.

When we first moved into the house, we continued allowing Daniel to fall asleep on the couch in the living room. After he was asleep for a little while, either Simon or I would carry him to his bed. After having a few days where he woke up and had trouble getting back to sleep, we changed tactics. I started putting him to sleep in his own bed. He didn't want to sleep by himself, so I began sleeping with him until he fell asleep.

Some nights, I was so tired that I fell asleep before him, and I didn't wake until the middle of the night to use the bathroom.

I continued sleeping with Daniel, but eventually we were able to get him to sleep by himself, in his own bed. He insisted on having the lights on, but after a while, we were able to get him to sleep in the dark. It was another achievement, and although progress was slow, the important thing was that there was progress. Much of this was because of respite and because of his regular weekend stays. Although respite ended up causing a lot of anxiety for him, it did help greatly with his development.

Eight

As promised, we started receiving regular respite and, as suspected, found it was only a band-aid solution. A support worker came to the house at nine a.m. every Saturday and stayed until noon. Simon and I took Jessica out, while the support worker stayed at the house with Daniel. As it was only three hours, it wasn't enough time to watch a movie, so we normally went out for coffee and shopping. Jessica and I ate, while Simon, who couldn't be persuaded to have anything else, had coffee. The three hours flew by, and no one looked forward to returning home. A mess in the kitchen normally waited for us at home, and Daniel was hungry and very irritable. As he had little interest in toys, the staff usually allowed him to 'cook' in the kitchen. As he hadn't eaten, our priority was always to try to get him to eat something. Saturday afternoons dragged by, and the relaxing effect of respite wore off within a few minutes of coming home.

We had our first respite weekend booked and were eagerly counting down the days until we had a whole weekend to ourselves. The respite was scheduled for the last weekend of the school holidays. Even with the nine days of holiday care, and three hours weekly of respite, the six week holidays were dragging on and were painfully slow. We were exhausted and wondered how we had coped in Sydney where we didn't receive any respite, and the holiday program was for two days only. Daniel's behaviour was getting worse instead of better, and Simon and I were burnt out.

Daniel's first weekend stay was booked for the last weekend of January. On Thursday, he woke up with his jaw swollen to three times its normal size, and we took him straight to the emergency department. After a lengthy wait, we were seen by a doctor, who discovered the cause.

Daniel had an abscess in his mouth and several infected baby teeth. The abscess would need to be drained and the infected teeth would need to be extracted. He would also be put on a course of antibiotics to treat the infection. Due to his severe autism, it was decided the abscess and teeth would have to be dealt with while he was under general anaesthetic. The surgery was booked for the following day.

We were taken to the children's ward where Daniel and I would be staying. I was allowed to stay in his room, as he would not have been able to cope by himself. The surgery was scheduled for Friday at ten a.m. and went ahead without incident. He recovered well from the anaesthetic, but it was decided he should stay in hospital for a few days to help him get over the infection. While we were staying in the hospital, I met another mother who also had a difficult child. She mentioned that her child was on medication to help with his behaviour. Her child was slightly younger than Daniel, and she claimed the medication had made the child's behaviour much more manageable. She also told me it helped with the child's sleeping. I desperately wanted Daniel's behaviour to be less severe and raised the possibility of trying medication when the paediatrician did his rounds.

The paediatrician was a lovely, elderly gentleman who seemed to be genuinely interested in all the patients at the hospital. He greeted Daniel warmly. 'How's my favourite little boy?' he asked.

As Daniel couldn't speak, he quickly turned his attention to me. I told the paediatrician about his behavioural issues and his severe constipation and asked if Daniel could be given medication to moderate his behaviour. He listened patiently but he wanted other interventions and behavioural therapies to be tried before medication was considered. I was desperate for medication for him, but the paediatrician was adamant that he was too young. I also asked about the cause of his severe constipation. He dismissed any possibility that the constipation had any cause other than physiological. He did this without any sort of abdominal examination or testing and suggested we try fibre supplements and a stool softener. He finished his consultation, and I was left feeling disgruntled and frustrated. As I sat stewing and dwelling on how we were going to cope with Daniel, I heard the paediatrician asking the next patient, 'How's my favourite little boy?'

Simon came with Jessica to visit on the weekend. He had cancelled the weekend respite and had booked Jessica into daycare for the additional week days. With just Jessica in his care, Simon was relaxed and well rested. He bought ice cream for Daniel and we mixed a stool softener and antibiotics into the ice cream. He couldn't swallow tablets at that stage. There was no other way to give Daniel the laxative, as I didn't want to risk putting him off any other food. He was still an incredibly finicky eater and getting him to eat was a constant battle. Like many battles, it was a losing one, and Daniel was very thin and small for his age.

While at the hospital, Daniel was seen by a number of paediatricians. I asked one of them for his opinion on the severity of his autism. He was reluctant to answer but eventually admitted that his autism was severe. It didn't come as a surprise but, nevertheless, it wasn't easy to hear.

I persisted with asking for medication for Daniel. I was so desperate I even admitted that Simon and I really couldn't cope with him. I thought if the paediatrician and hospital staff knew how desperate the situation was, they would try some medication for him. I wanted something that would take the edge off his behaviour, help him sleep and just make him more manageable. I was willing to say and do anything to get the help we needed for Daniel. When I told the staff I didn't want to take him home because I couldn't cope with him, they advised me that they would have to call Child Services. I didn't have any objections to Child Services being contacted.

Once at home, we received a visit from Child Services. The case workers did a brief inspection of our house and complimented me on having such a beautiful, clean and tidy house. They interviewed me and determined very quickly that Daniel wasn't in any danger and was in a loving and caring home. They told me that he would never be taken away from us, unless things drastically changed. They also explained the process if Simon and I ever had to surrender Daniel. Simon was called at work, and Child Services interviewed him over the phone. They didn't see or meet Daniel at all. In spite of the bad publicity surrounding Child Services, I found the case workers to be polite, professional and very respectful to Simon and me.

As well as Child Services, we also received a visit from two case workers from Disability Services. After introductions were made, Simon and I completed an assessment on Daniel. It was very similar to the previous assessments that we had done for speech therapy and respite. It took about ninety minutes and left us feeling drained, frustrated and depressed. We discussed his behavioural issues, as well as the difficulties we were having with his eating, sleeping and bowel movements. The conversation flowed freely until solutions were discussed.

There weren't any solutions. We were told we could apply for more respite but, without funding, we wouldn't receive more. We couldn't get funding, as it was allocated twice a year, in December and again in July.

Agitated by this information, I said, 'But the staff at the hospital told me to apply for funding. It took me forever to complete the application, and it was rejected. Why was I told to apply in January?'

'I don't know,' one of the workers replied.

This response angered me even more.

'You can try to apply again in June,' the worker said to try to appease me. 'It's very unlikely that you will get extra funding. Funds are very limited and there are cases that are much more severe. The funding will be allocated to those people who really need it.'

We weren't given any more information about these more severe cases. Perhaps we might have been more understanding, possibly even agreeable, had such information been given. Referrals for both speech therapy and behavioural therapy were made, as well as a recommendation to continue with respite. We were advised that there would be waiting periods involved, as there were more severe cases. They made it clear that we were not a priority case.

It was obvious that Disability Services weren't going to help us and we would have to help ourselves. It was frustrating, and being told repeatedly that there were other much more severe cases fuelled my repressed anger. It took my hatred for people who worked in disability to another level, as it felt like the only people they helped were themselves. It didn't assist to be told about other families who received much more respite than we did. We heard this information from support workers and, although the information was never confirmed, it still angered me. The only thing that came from our hospital stay was that the paediatrician had agreed to see Daniel at the school clinic.

We continued to mix the stool softener into Daniel's ice cream and he continued to suffer from constipation. After he started refusing ice cream, we stopped using it, as it had only caused him to have wind. After one particularly long interval between bowel movements, Simon took matters into his own hands. One evening, unbeknown to me, he gave Daniel laxatives. He didn't give him the recommended amount, which was one to two squares, but gave him six squares. In the morning, we woke up to a horrendous stench. It didn't take long to discover the source of the odour.

The carpet in Daniel's room was covered in diarrhoea and the smell was revolting. He had pooed at least once in his bed sometime during the night. In the morning, when he got out of bed, it had dripped down his pyjama pants and onto the carpet. From the amount of diarrhoea on the carpet, he may have soiled himself again after he woke up. It was all over his legs, bottom and pyjama pants as well as his bed and carpet. Hours of carpet cleaning, an open window, clean bedding and a can of disinfectant left his room smelling marginally better. The whole house smelt horrible for almost a month.

Every month seemed to bring a new problem that caused frustration for Daniel and stress for everyone else in the family. Unfortunately, the problems tended to last much longer than a month and, unlike the 'word of the month', accumulated instead of being replaced. The problems weren't limited to our home and happened at school, respite and in the car. Whenever he got upset, we referred to it as 'Daniel getting broken'.

He got broken frequently and we all blamed one another for breaking him. A lot of the time, Daniel broke himself.

One weekend, to try to help Daniel deal with his phobia of planes, Simon took him out to the backyard and showed him the plane that we had just heard. After that, every time he heard a plane, he ran out to the backyard to see it. If he didn't see the plane, he had a major meltdown. This routine happened so quickly that Simon and I were reluctant to try anything new, for fear of the ongoing impact it would have. We started to double think everything we did, and we were all walking on eggshells. More than ever, we relied on respite.

As we felt that we weren't getting the most out of respite, we changed the respite routine. We requested that the support worker take Daniel out for three hours, while we relaxed at home. He loved going out, and looked forward to a support worker coming to the house. As caring for the disabled is extremely difficult, the staff turnover was exceedingly high. There were some workers who Daniel preferred over others, and he took a real shine to one young man. For reasons only known to him, he called the worker Joe. It wasn't his name, but Daniel always called this young man and every other support worker Joe. The new arrangement worked better, as Daniel got to go out, while Simon and I caught up on jobs around the house. I was finally able to vacuum my house in peace. The only people inconvenienced by the new respite were the support workers

Unfortunately, the respite service turned out to be only marginally more reliable than Daniel's taxi service. By this stage, I understood the principal's frustration with the taxi service, as, on many occasions, it would not show up in the morning. This agitated Daniel and put him in a bad mood for school. The taxi service proved so unreliable that we cancelled it. When Simon started working night shift, he also started taking Daniel to school and picking him up in the afternoon.

Since respite was scheduled for Saturday, if a support worker didn't show up, I couldn't call the office, which was closed during the weekends. A no-show for respite also put Daniel in a bad mood. To avoid his disappointment, we began telling him about respite only after we saw a car pull up in the driveway. This usually meant taking him to the bathroom at the last minute.

One Saturday, before respite, Simon took Daniel to the bathroom and used the bathroom directly after him. After that, Daniel wanted to be in the bathroom when anyone else used it. Both Simon and I allowed him to be with us but told Jessica to sneak to the bathroom whenever she needed to go. We mentioned this bathroom issue at one of our regular individual education plan meetings. The teacher organised a meeting for us with the occupational therapist, to discuss the bathroom problem and numerous other issues that we were having with him.

Although Daniel was happy to wear long pants, jumpers and closed-in shoes in Sydney and in his first winter in Queensland, he now refused. He wouldn't wear socks, closed-in shoes, jumpers or even long-sleeved shirts. He also continued to wear his shorts without any underwear. We weren't overly fussed by the underwear at that stage, as we felt that there were more pressing issues to be resolved. It was July, and although we were in Queensland, the weather was cold enough that a jumper, long pants and closed-in shoes were needed. Daniel was also very thin and tended to feel the cold.

We mentioned our concerns about Daniel's inappropriate clothing to the occupational therapist. Like a lot of therapists we had dealt with in the past, she was very informative as to why Daniel and other autistic children wouldn't wear appropriate clothing. She wasn't, however, informative about how to get him to wear clothes suited to the weather. At home, he draped a pink blanket around his shoulders to keep warm. The blanket draped down his back and resembled a king's cloak. As all of our attempts to have him wear a jumper failed dismally, we conceded and let him take his blanket to school. It kept him warm and made him very easy to spot in the playground.

At the meeting, we also spoke about the issue of Daniel wanting to be in the bathroom with us. The occupational therapist made no reference to other autistic children doing this, and for the first, but not last, time, Simon and I were beginning to understand the severity and uniqueness of Daniel's autism. The therapist suggested saying no when he wanted to come into the bathroom and rewarding him with Skittles after he had allowed us to use the bathroom by ourselves. We tried her method for one, very long week and then gave up. We couldn't deal with the tantrums this method caused and didn't think it was worth the additional stress. In the end, Simon and I also began sneaking to the bathroom. Eventually, Daniel outgrew this behaviour on his own, and we were able to use the bathroom in peace.

I finished my teacher aide certificate three and, although I was unable to find work as a teacher aide, I did find part-time work in banking. It was around this time that Simon reduced his night shift hours from full time to part time. Daniel's behaviour hadn't improved, and Simon was becoming increasingly exhausted from working night shift. Tired from work, Simon usually came home to an angry and agitated Daniel throwing a tantrum in the garage. We were now regularly having Daniel stay weekends at respite. The weekend stays gave us a much-needed break but weren't something that Daniel enjoyed. He threw a tantrum when we left him at the house, and seeing tears stream down his face as he watched us drive away broke our hearts. Eventually, we asked the respite service to pick Daniel up from his special school on a Friday afternoon. The respite service wasn't meant to take him until four p.m. but agreed, as the service also picked up other children from his school. We thought having him picked up from his school on a Friday was kinder and easier on everyone. We were mistaken.

Nine

Simon's dad passed away in October 2008. Although he had been unwell since 1992, we were still unprepared for his passing. Simon insisted on going by himself to Sydney for the funeral. I still regret not going to Sydney with him and giving him the support he needed.

Unfortunately, life didn't pause for Simon, and so he didn't grieve, or deal with his dad's death. As his dad was the only family member Simon felt close to, his passing away left Simon feeling completely alone. He sank further into depression, and shut me and the rest of the world out. Although he never stopped loving Jessica and Daniel, I felt he only barely tolerated me. We bickered constantly and our arguments would often remain unresolved. Whenever I asked Simon how he was or how his day was, his reply was always the same.

'Shit!'

He never expanded, so a stony silence usually followed.

'How can I help you?' I constantly asked. 'What can I do? What would you do? I don't know what to do. I want to help you, but I don't know how.'

'Figure it out for yourself. What would I do? I would do whatever it takes – whatever it takes. You don't do anything because you don't care.' Frustrated and angry, his reply remained consistent.

I couldn't convince him that I cared, no matter how hard I tried. Fed up from getting nowhere, and convinced that I was only making the situation worse, I stopped asking.

We plodded on and continued to try to go out as a family. Our outings often only consisted of taking Daniel to the video shop or for an ice cream. It was still more than we managed in Sydney, so although it was slow, it was still progress.

Daniel developed an obsession with one particular street in our area, and we went to that street at least once a week. His obsession was so strong that, at home, he incorporated the name of the street when singing along to popular songs. He also used Google Maps to look at his street and continued to do so, even after we left Queensland.

Although Daniel's vocabulary had increased, his language was used more for his entertainment than communication and wasn't always appropriate. To help with transitioning from one activity to another, teachers had taught him to say 'Bye' to an activity or object. As a result, he said 'Bye' to all inanimate objects. He did it at home, as well as anytime we took him out. He didn't have any volume control, and his loud farewells attracted unwanted attention.

As our outings were short, boredom was still an issue. To keep the boredom at bay and to entertain Daniel, we made up all sorts of silly games and songs. One of the games we played was 'the flying game'. It involved either Simon or me lying on our back, with our legs and arms in the air, not unlike a dead dog. Daniel would stand in front of us, and we would lift him up and hold him over our body. He was eight but so tiny and light that holding him up wasn't difficult. His fearless nature meant he loved the game and would ask to play it all the time. When he wanted to play it he said, 'Go for a fly.'

We also used the game to encourage him to use his words to communicate. We were still hopeful that, if his communication improved, his behaviour would also improve and he would throw fewer tantrums.

Tantrums were still frequent and intense and happened over the smallest things. Spilling a drink was something that always caused a major meltdown. Having food on someone's face was also something that Daniel really struggled with. There were at least a hundred other things that caused tantrums, most of which couldn't be successfully avoided. There were also tantrums that occurred regularly out of the blue, for reasons that were unknown to anyone other than him.

At our appointments held at Daniel's special school, Simon and I constantly asked for medication to help deal with his tantrums. The paediatrician finally relented and started him on a medication commonly prescribed for autistic children, called Endep. He warned us that the medication was not the 'silver bullet' we were hoping for.

The paediatrician's warning fell on deaf ears, and once at home, we immediately mixed the prescription medication into Daniel's ice cream. We eagerly awaited improvements in his behaviour, mood, appetite and sleep. After a week, there wasn't any improvement; if anything, he seemed even more agitated and irritable than usual. It was a huge disappointment and, against my better judgement, I tried the medication myself. It left me feeling tired, agitated and very depressed. I couldn't stand the way it made me feel, so when he refused to eat his ice cream, we didn't continue with his medication.

The paediatrician agreed to try a low dose of Ritalin, more commonly used for children with attention deficit hyperactivity disorder (ADHD). We were hopeful that it would help improve Daniel's behaviour. It had absolutely no effect. This time, both Simon and I tried one of the Ritalin tablets. It didn't just enhance our mood. It left us happy, energised and feeling on top of the world. It made his lack of reaction to the medication even harder to accept. The search for medication continued.

The paediatrician was incredibly supportive and patient, and continued to trial other medication for Daniel. The next medication we tried was a low dosage of Clozapine. Again, we mixed the correct dose into his ice cream and waited to see what effect, if any, the medication would have. Like the other medications we had tried previously, this one seemed to have no effect. By this stage, it felt like Daniel was immune to any medication that the paediatrician was willing to prescribe.

In spite of the medication not having any effect on Daniel, we continued to give it to him. One Sunday afternoon, he was unusually quiet. This quiet aroused our suspicion, and we started looking around the house to find out what he was up to. We searched the house and couldn't find him anywhere. It was Jessica who found him.

We had a small garden shed in the corner of the backyard, and he was standing on the roof of the garden shed. He was standing dangerously close to the edge. 'Go for a fly,' he said when he saw us.

We managed to get him down safely and moved the compost bin so he couldn't climb on the roof again. We also immediately stopped the medication. It may have simply been Daniel's natural tendency to climb, or his fearless attitude, but we stopped the medication anyway.

After being let down by both Disability Services Queensland (DSQ) and medication, I continued to try to find ways of helping Daniel. I requested testing, with the hope that the severity of his autism and intellectual impairment might entitle us to more assistance from DSQ. Although the report showed that Daniel's developmental delay was severe, we didn't receive any additional help. I also agreed to speak with a guidance counsellor at his school. The session lasted for an hour and did not help me at all.

We were still being told fairly regularly that there were many other people much worse off than us. In spite of the severity of Daniel's autism and behaviour, we were generally treated as whiners. We weren't treated with respect; the issues we faced were not taken seriously, and we weren't getting help from anyone. I was told, regularly, that I was negative. My negative attitude and unwillingness to repeatedly try things that hadn't worked previously were blamed for his poor, almost non-existent progress. It irked me, but not nearly as much as the assumption that experts understood him and his capabilities much better than I did.

I continued being the 'squeaky wheel' with the hope of one day getting some 'oil'. I was disliked and did not care at all, as the feeling was mutual. Many meetings with professionals started with introductions and then followed with one of the professionals saying, 'Unfortunately, we don't have a silver bullet.' Every time I heard that statement, I saw red, and, unfortunately, I heard it often. I don't know if it was the frequency of the statement, its pointlessness, or the smugness that usually accompanied it. It was not a good way to start meetings.

The meetings, in general, were a complete waste of time. I usually felt drained, frustrated and highly agitated by the end of them. The professionals were great at providing explanations for Daniel's behaviour but didn't actually have any practical solutions for us. We were desperate for help, but help continued to elude us.

Meanwhile, Simon continued to struggle with both his eating disorder and depression. I wanted to help, but had no idea how to help him. After my frustrations trying to get help with Daniel, the only thing I knew was I didn't want any professional help. I didn't want Simon to have anything permanently on his record that would hamper future job opportunities. I didn't want to make things worse, so unfortunately I didn't do anything. Understandably, Simon interpreted my reluctance to seek professional help as a complete and utter lack of caring on my part. Nothing was further from the truth, but Simon refused to believe that I loved and cared for him. He felt isolated and unloved. He turned to medication to help with his sleep issues, depression, anxiety and anger. The medication didn't help, and he continued to battle on.

Jessica started year one, and, as I was still only working three days a week, I continued to volunteer in her classroom.

One morning, when Simon was dropping Jessica and me at school, he looked at me and said, 'If you don't go to Jessica's class today, I'll make it worth your while.'

I was both intrigued and hopeful, so quickly called the school to let them know I wouldn't be in. Simon and I went to breakfast. I expected him to order a coffee while I ordered food, as that is what normally happened. Simon ordered and ate food. It felt like a miracle, and I was so happy, tears began to prick my eyes. I had wanted him to eat for so long, and now it was finally happening.

As we ate breakfast, Simon said, 'I can't keep doing this ridiculous diet any more. I'm sick of it. I'm hungry, I'm tired and I'm cold all the time. I've had enough and it's not fair on you and the kids. You guys shouldn't have to put up with me being angry all of the time.'

'Yay! Now more eating, less talking,' I replied, happy and overwhelmed.

He took my hand from across the table, squeezed it gently and said,

'Don't worry. I intend to eat. Don't you worry about that. I'm so sorry for the way I've treated you. I'm sorry you've had to put up with so much crap. I really do love you, you know, and I'm going to make it up to you. You and the kids.'

It was the happiest I had seen him in a long time, and the first time in what felt like forever that he showed me affection and love. It was wonderful and I was on cloud nine. In the last month or so, he had begun experiencing an odd numbness in his fingers. When he wasn't able to play the guitar any more, he decided enough was enough.

Like any person who has deprived themselves of food for a long time, Simon binged. He ate all the food he had been craving but denying himself, for over four years. The floodgates opened, and he gorged himself to the point of being sick. We made the most of his eating and went out for lunch, dinner and dessert at every possible opportunity. We food shopped like crazy and tried all the takeaways. We also went away for a weekend to Brisbane. Unlike other weekends away, where he stuck to his diet, we all indulged. It was the best weekend we ever had. Simon was deliriously happy, and so was I.

After our weekend away, unfortunately Simon returned to a new marginally improved diet. It had been a crazy, fun and food-filled fortnight. I agreed that Simon couldn't continue eating the way he had been, but wanted him to follow a more sensible diet. I wanted him to eat toast and cereal for breakfast, sandwiches or rolls for lunch, and a sensible-sized meal for dinner. I wanted him to snack on a variety of fruit, and treat himself to desserts, chocolates, take always et cetera regularly. My sensible advice fell on deaf ears. Simon chose to eat two small bowls of cornflakes for breakfast, two small bowls of cornflakes for lunch and a children's size meal for dinner, followed by another two small bowls of cornflakes for dessert. It wasn't enough, and it left him so hungry that he started eating his lunch at nine-thirty.

He also bought a bike and started going for excessively long bike rides. It wasn't long before his weight once again started to drop. When his weight eventually plateaued, he took up jogging. He started slowly, but gradually increased his run to over three kilometres. He continued with the daily weighing ritual that caused so many arguments and gave him so much anxiety. I was frustrated and defeated. He was hungry all the time and angry nearly all of the time. We plodded on

Boredom remained an issue for Daniel, and a meeting at the school one day summed up the situation nicely. The teacher was going through his timetable with us, showing us all the activities that he did at school. It was suggested that it might be a good idea to try using a similar timetable at home during the upcoming holidays. Simon and I agreed, it sounded like a good idea, but unfortunately, the only activity we had on Daniel's school holiday timetable was 'wake up'. After that, it was nothing but blank space until bedtime.

To kill time and keep boredom at bay, we decided to try bike riding as a family. The local council had recently installed a bike path that was very close to our house. We thought it would be a safe activity that we could all enjoy. We bought bikes for Jessica and me, and a trike for Daniel, as we hadn't managed to teach him to ride a bike. As he was still scared of dogs, they were inevitably an issue. One day, while on a bike ride, we came across a man walking two Maltese dogs. Daniel stopped. Petrified, he hopped off his trike and refused to get back on. Simon stayed with a nervous and agitated Daniel, while I approached the man.

'Hi, how's it going?' I said.

'Good. Yourself?' he replied.

'What gorgeous dogs. I love dogs.'

'Thank you. This little guy is Harley and this little guy is Davis. You can pat them if you like. They're pretty friendly, and they love attention. They're really just a pair of big sooks.'

'My son's really scared of dogs,' I said, as I started patting the dogs. 'Would you mind if I try to get him to pat these little guys? It might help.'

'No, not at all,' he replied.

I continued patting the dogs and, after a lot of coaxing, Daniel started patting them too. He wasn't scared and even seemed to like them.

He wasn't as scared of dogs after that but was still just as irritated by the sound of dogs barking.

Dogs, unfortunately, weren't the only issue we dealt with while riding our bikes. To get to the bike path, we had to ride on the street near the road, for about five hundred metres. As Daniel didn't have any road sense at all, even this short distance proved stressful. He didn't ride his trike in a straight line or keep to the left. Usually, Simon or I rode beside him, as it was easier than trying to correct him. Anytime we asked him to keep to the left, he became very agitated.

He also needed to stop and rest frequently, as his trike was quite heavy and tiring to ride. There were benches along the bike path, but Daniel wanted to rest wherever he felt tired. He preferred grass to the benches and insisted that we all stop and rest with him. He also insisted that we all remove our bike helmets every time we stopped. He referred to the helmets as 'motorbike'. He repeated, 'Take my motorbike' or 'Goin' to take my motorbike', until we took off our helmets. He didn't take no for an answer. To keep the peace, we took our helmets off.

As Daniel's speech was developing, he started greeting people whom we met on the bike path. The way he referred to people wasn't always politically correct. All people, regardless of age or gender, were referred to as 'grandma'. He also referred to all Asian people as 'fried rice' and indigenous Australians as 'boomerang'. We don't know how he came up with these names, and we always corrected him. They weren't lessons easily learnt, in spite of our ongoing efforts. We apologised to many people. We were fortunate in that everyone we encountered was very understanding and accepting.

Daniel was also very affectionate to women who resembled or were similar in age to his grandmothers. He wanted to hug any woman who reminded him of them. Although he loves my dad dearly and also loved Simon's dad, he didn't do this with men. Again, we constantly corrected him and apologised frequently. Luckily, no one took offence at his affectionate hugs, and everyone we encountered was very understanding and tolerant.

While on our bike rides, Daniel also developed an obsession with driveways. He wanted to ride up people's driveways, and then slowly reverse his trike back down. We assumed that he was imitating a car reversing down the driveway. We didn't allow him to go on other people's driveways, so he threw tantrums and became highly agitated. Eventually, we rode our bikes less and less, until we stopped. We continued to go on bike rides while he was at respite.

As medication hadn't helped with Daniel's behaviour, we tried a behaviour management program. The Evolve program started in July 2011 and went for approximately three months. It involved a lengthy assessment and observations of Daniel in his classroom, as well as interviews with his teacher and Simon and me. It didn't help us at all, and the only result was a detailed, though not entirely accurate, report.

The report mentioned that Daniel had frequent, intense tantrums at home and school. It also implied that he previously needed to have 'time out' several times during the school day. Time out involved him sitting outside the classroom on a small bench. The report mentioned his tendencies to lash out at other people, and to run off from his teachers and the class group. The report also made note of the fact that on outings with the school, he sometimes required two adults to restrain him. It mentioned that both Simon and I were unsure how much longer we would be able to continue caring for him. In spite of all this information, the report concluded with a description of Daniel as a calm and quiet eleven-year-old. There were other inaccuracies that made me wonder if the case worker was even listening when I answered all of those tedious assessment questions.

Like all assessments, the one for Evolve was time-consuming and very thorough. It was a blanket assessment, and the assessor insisted on asking every question. She filled in the form and wrote down any additional relevant information. Many of the questions were aimed at establishing how much assistance Daniel required with simple daily tasks. Some were focused around food.

'Can Daniel make a sandwich, or butter a piece of toast?' the assessor asked.

'Yes. But not really,' I replied. 'He can butter a piece of toast, but we do it for him. It's quicker, easier and a lot less messy. Daniel puts on way too much butter, makes holes in the bread and, by the time he's finished, the toast is stone cold, and we end up wasting it.'

She nodded and wrote a short sentence in her notepad.

After we had finished the assessment, worn out and fed up, I said, 'Sorry, but couldn't this assessment just have been emailed to me? I could have filled it out by myself and emailed it back to you.' Given how many times I had been told that there wasn't enough funding for disabled people, I thought it was a valid point.

'That's not our procedure,' she replied. 'Our procedure is for me to interview the parents and complete the form.'

I had asked the same question previously of other people who worked in disability and had received more or less the same reply.

About a month later, I read in the report, 'Daniel is capable of buttering toast independently.'

After the initial assessment, the case worker started coming to see me weekly. She came for an hour while Daniel was at school, and we spoke about him, his behaviour and the case worker's children. As she only came to the house while he was at school, she didn't ever see, or experience any of his behaviours or outbursts. She was very informative and able to provide explanations for many of his behavioural issues but didn't really have any solutions for these. As Daniel was at school, I assumed the program hadn't actually started.

'When is the program going to start?' I asked, one morning.

'This is the program,' she replied, somewhat taken aback by my question.

The program finished shortly after that, and we continued to struggle with Daniel's behaviour.

Fortunately, Daniel had a young, energetic, enthusiastic teacher who had a real passion for teaching and helping disabled children. In spite of our initial doubts, this teacher was the first one willing to take Daniel on a school camp. With his teacher and the help of a lovely, patient and experienced teacher aide, Daniel coped with three days and two nights away on camp. He had a wonderful time and experienced many things which Simon and I wouldn't have thought possible.

While we were waiting to pick him up from camp, we started speaking to the other parents who were also waiting for their children. There had been a storm the previous evening.

'How does Daniel cope with storms?' one mum asked. 'Luke hates them.'

In spite of being scared of almost all loud noises, Daniel wasn't scared of storms. This changed soon after that conversation, and we added another thing to his long list of phobias.

Daniel's teacher was willing to try anything with him and even took him to a movie with the rest of his class. He didn't sit still at home while watching TV and didn't like the dark. So we didn't think he would be able to cope with a movie. The communication book summed up the outing with the comment, 'We survived.' Even though the movie wasn't a success, it was still commendable that his teacher was so willing to try to help him.

The teacher was also able to get Daniel to brush his teeth at school, as well as wear underwear, socks and closed-in shoes. The underwear, socks and shoes were taken off the minute he came home and were only worn during school hours. At home, he still wore his shorts without anything on underneath them. Eventually, Simon was able to get him to wear the shoes to school. It was another small step forward.

We didn't have many unexpected visitors, and we were surprised when the doorbell rang one Sunday afternoon. Simon answered it, and found two ladies and a young girl at the door. The ladies had Bibles and religious pamphlets in their hands and were going from door to door to spread the word of the Lord. They introduced themselves, including the little girl, who was about three or four. After hearing the ladies speaking, Daniel ran to the door. Simon introduced Daniel, who was happy and intrigued to see visitors.

The ladies found him charming, and said, 'Aren't you a lovely boy. What a handsome boy.'

'Thank you,' Simon replied.

'Have you been fortunate enough to witness God's glorious gifts?' one of the ladies asked, turning her attention back to Simon.

Before Simon had a chance to answer, Daniel dropped his shorts to his ankles. Fortunately, one of the ladies had lightning-quick reflexes, and her hand covered the young girl's eyes almost immediately.

'I'm sorry. I'm really sorry,' said a stunned Simon as he quickly pulled up Daniel's shorts.

'That's fine,' one of the embarrassed ladies muttered, as they made a hasty exit.

We weren't visited by them or anyone else spreading the word of the Lord ever again.

The school year ended, and the challenge of entertaining Daniel for six weeks began. For Christmas 2011, we bought him an iPad. Simon installed a number of apps that he thought Daniel would like. They were mostly balloon, music and plane apps. Daniel also used the iPad to watch YouTube. He watched the *Wiggles*, *Hi Five* and several other children's shows. He also enjoyed watching children getting haircuts, getting needles and throwing tantrums. Daniel's iPad was a constant source of background noise and our house was seldom, if ever, quiet.

Daniel proved to be very apt at using his iPad and used it all day every day. It was sometimes a source of frustration, but for the most part, it was a blessing. Earlier in the year, his teacher had let me know that there was an organisation that gave iPads to disabled children. I wrote the required letter and filled in the lengthy paperwork. It was a long process but, unfortunately, we were unsuccessful. We were never given any explanation.

Ten

Unfortunately, Daniel had to change teachers and classes every year. In 2012, he had a new teacher. This teacher was a mature lady who didn't have the same enthusiasm and energy as his previous teacher. With a new teacher, class and classroom, his behaviour declined and his anxiety increased. The progress he made with his previous teacher was rapidly undone. Even though he didn't finish school until three p.m., his new teacher requested that we pick him up at two-forty-five p.m. It wasn't convenient, as Jessica didn't finish until three p.m. We accommodated her and started picking him up earlier.

Something Daniel had been prone to, from a very young age, was regular fits of uncontrollable laughter. These were completely out of the blue and could happen anywhere and everywhere, but particularly at the dinner table. We spoke to another parent at his school whose child did the same. When questioned about why they were laughing, both children just replied, 'Laughing'. We were none the wiser, but not overly fussed, as there were so many other more pressing issues to deal with.

One day, Daniel's teacher mentioned that she thought the laughing fits were actually mini-seizures. I brushed the comment off, in my typical arrogant way, but Simon took it to heart. It was something else for him to worry about, and it was a long, anxious wait until our next appointment with the paediatrician. The laughing fits turned out to be nothing to be concerned about. The paediatrician confirmed that Daniel didn't have epilepsy, and that his laughing fits weren't mini-seizures. As we both felt we weren't getting anything from these appointments, we cancelled future visits. The paediatrician retired shortly after, due to mounting pressure from the local hospital.

I didn't hold a high opinion of Daniel's teacher and after attending a morning tea in the classroom, thought even less of her. After the morning tea, the children sat at a small table to have their lunch. Daniel didn't eat anything, and I was surprised to see that neither teacher nor teacher aide made any effort to encourage him to eat. I was also surprised to see how little supervision there was while the children were seated at the table.

At the school, there were two meetings a year, with at least one parent required to attend both meetings. There was a meeting to discuss the student's school report, and another meeting to discuss the student's individual education plan. Parents were required to attend both meetings, based on the idea that parents should have some input into their child's education. During one of his IEP meetings, his teacher told me about an incident that involved Daniel trying to stab another child with a fork while they were seated at the lunch table.

I was sorely tempted to say, 'It wouldn't have happened if you did your job and actually supervised them.' To be polite, I bit my tongue, and we continued. The meeting was held in the classroom and when it was interrupted to allow his teacher to take a personal call, I was able to observe a lesson.

There were five children in the classroom, including Daniel. One child walked around the room touching things. Daniel sat and glared at that student, who continued walking around. Neither teacher nor teacher aide made any attempt to correct that student or encourage the student to sit down. Another two children sat staring vacantly ahead, neither child looking at the aide. The fifth child was happy and laughing while rocking her body back and forward. In spite of the fact that she didn't have the attention of a single student, the teacher aide went ahead with the lesson.

The purpose of an IEP is to discuss your child's behavioural issues and establish short-term and long-term goals. We resumed the meetingd.

'What would you like Daniel's goals to be this year?' his teacher asked.

'I think the most important thing is to focus on improving his behaviour. I would love to see him throwing fewer tantrums and just be easier to deal with. That's all I want,' I replied.

'That's good but we need to focus on academics. I would like Daniel's goals to be learning to count, writing his name and identifying different colours,' his teacher said.

'That's pointless,' I said. 'It's not going to help Daniel or Simon and me. We need to concentrate on helping Daniel with his communication and help him manage his anxiety. If he can really start to communicate and manage his anxiety, he's going to be more independent and have a better quality of life. If he behaves better, we'll be able to take him out more and do other things with him. If we can improve his communication, he'll be able to tell us what he wants. We won't be guessing what he wants and he'll be less frustrated. How would you even know that he understands what you're trying to teach him? He might just repeat everything you say. And if he does understand, do you really think knowing colours is actually going to help him?'

'The Board of Education wants all special schools to focus on academics instead of life skills,' she said, completely ignoring my question.

I didn't ask if anyone from the Board of Education ever observed any lessons being taught at the school. My own opinion was that his teacher was more interested in making her job easier than in helping Daniel. I chose to keep this opinion to myself. I conceded, and academic goals were included in Daniel's IEP. We concluded the meeting, and I went home, another pointless meeting done.

His new teacher elected not to take Daniel's class on camp. No explanation was given. I didn't see any point putting in a complaint about it and just let the matter slide. I wasn't happy about it but was worried that a complaint would negatively affect the way his teacher treated him.

Although it had been a disappointing school year, Daniel started to make progress with both his speech and communication. His vocabulary increased, and he started using speech to communicate his needs and wants. He didn't start with 'yes' or 'no', but started with the word 'finished', which was accompanied by a frantic waving back and forward of one or both of his thumbs. He used the word 'finished' or 'We put away', anytime there was something that he didn't like or want. A lot of his speech was echolalia. He repeated phrases that he heard throughout his day, either at school or respite. A lot of it was aimed at no one, and he often spoke to empty space. Although his communication was improving, his anxiety was increasing, and he was often very agitated.

He also started saying, 'I want Daniel' when he wanted something. Unfortunately, knowing what he did or didn't want wasn't as helpful as we hoped it would be, as he often wanted things that we couldn't give him. Although he wasn't keen on large animals, he loved insects, frogs, lizards and, in particular, geckos. We were always very careful not to say anything whenever we saw a gecko, in case he heard us. If he saw a gecko, he always said, 'I want Daniel.' Geckos are fast and difficult to catch but, with practice, it was something I eventually mastered.

Daniel loved holding and playing with insects and other small animals. He loved frogs, grasshoppers and any other little bugs he happened to find. One evening while I was putting him to sleep, I noticed a large cockroach. It was on one of his bedroom walls but too high for me to reach. I continued working on the computer and kept an eye on Daniel, as well as the cockroach. My plan was to kill the roach once it was low enough. I kept working and, even though I continually checked on the roach, I managed to lose track of it. I started looking around the room and checked the walls as well as the carpet. I couldn't find it and assumed that it had gone to another room. I was relieved it was gone. I looked over at Daniel to see if he had fallen asleep. He was wide awake and quite happily playing with the roach.

Daniel still loved going out, and one of the first things he started saying was, 'Go for a drive.' He also started to understand more of what Simon, Jessica and I were saying. Unfortunately, it was still a case of one step forward, two steps back. Now that he was able to understand more of what we were saying, we had to speak very carefully. Anytime anyone said, 'Go for it,' Daniel said, 'Go for a drive.'

We couldn't mention my parents at all in front of Daniel, as he would expect them to be waiting at the front door. Initially, we tried spelling words we didn't want to say in front of him. This agitated him, and he responded in turn by spelling his own word. The word he spelt was always 'KOPO'. We have never understood how or why he chose those particular letters. As spelling words irritated him, we soon stopped doing it. There were many words that we couldn't say, and we started to watch our Ps and Qs, as well as walk on eggshells.

The word that caused the biggest issue was 'respite'. Although respite helped enormously with Daniel's behaviour, it was clear that he didn't enjoy it. It was the respite service that taught him to sit at a table, use a fork, hold hands with an adult in public, and swallow tablets. As he didn't enjoy respite, we couldn't say the word in front of him. We began referring to respite as 'R' as that didn't seem to bother him. He made it clear that he disliked respite stays, as when he returned he wanted his bag unpacked and put away immediately. He was also agitated and repeatedly said, 'Finished respite, we put the respite away.' We had to reassure him that he was staying home and that respite was 'finished'.

At that stage, Daniel was staying at the respite house about once a month. The frequency of stays increased his anxiety, as he didn't know when he was going into respite care. He didn't deal with the anxiety well and developed a highly irritating coping mechanism. He became obsessed with watching *Play School,* as it meant that he wasn't going to respite. When Simon picked him up from school, Daniel immediately needed constant reassurance that he wasn't going to respite. He repeated, 'We go home! We watch *Play School!*' It didn't matter how much Simon and I reassured him, he was relentless. It was worse if we tried to ignore him and didn't respond. He became highly agitated and aggressive. It was only a five-minute drive from school to our house, but he said, 'We go home, we watch *Play School*' in excess of thirty times. It was a loop that played every afternoon when we picked him up from school. It didn't end until he watched *Play School*. To ensure that we didn't miss the start of the program, Simon started recording it. We also kept at least one episode on the PVR, for the days when it wasn't on TV.

The other thing Daniel said was, 'School home, school home, school home, school home, school home, home home.' This was also repeated all day, every day. The only way to reassure and appease him was to say the words with him. He usually settled for a short time after we repeated this little mantra two or three times. We repeated it at least three times a day on a good day. On a bad day, it was an almost never ending loop. If we tried to ignore this behaviour, Daniel got very agitated. As always, we mentioned it to his teachers and a psychologist. The result was the same as on previous occasions that we asked for help. The reasons for the behaviour were explained, but no solutions were suggested.

The other thing we had to do was pack a bag for everyone when Daniel went into respite. It was something he insisted we did, as I think it made him feel better to think that he wasn't the only one going to respite. When he came home from school, he constantly checked his drawers to see if any of his clothes were missing. He was always suspicious that we might have packed his respite bag without his knowledge. He was suspicious, in spite of the fact that we always packed the bag with him.

Eleven

On Father's Day in 2012, we added a new furry member to the family. Fortunately, Daniel was delighted. He loved Penny, but having a dog didn't improve his behaviour or alleviate his anxiety at all. His anxiety wasn't limited to respite, and his fear of loud noises intensified. He was extremely scared of balloons, inflated and deflated, as well as anything else that could potentially pop. He was scared of chip packets, packets of biscuits, plastic bags and latex gloves. He was fine if he could hold the item but petrified if he couldn't. He needed to be in control, otherwise he would have a huge meltdown. He was also still scared of hand dryers, lawnmowers, any sort of power tools, starter guns used at school carnivals, loud cars and motorbikes. His anxiety led to control issues, and his need to control people and situations was prominent at both school and home.

At school, Daniel became obsessed with the classroom fans. He had to switch the fans on when he entered the classroom and switch them off when he left. He wanted to control the fans and his need for control became apparent in other ways too. One day at school, his class made some biscuits. While the biscuits were cooking, the children returned to the classroom. About fifteen minutes later, the teacher went back to the school kitchen to check on the biscuits. When she left, Daniel had a complete meltdown. Both his teacher and teacher aide were baffled by his outburst. Eventually, he calmed down enough for the staff to realise that he just wanted to see the biscuits the class had made.

Lunchtimes at school were particularly challenging for Daniel. If a child had a packet of chips or biscuits, Daniel ran from the lunch table and hid in the storage room at the back of the classroom. He was highly agitated and stood crying, while holding his hands firmly over his ears.

After a lot of reassurance, he was eventually persuaded to return to the lunch table. Sometimes he tried to take the packet from the other child. If they didn't comply, Daniel would hit the other child. He lashed out at others whenever he didn't get his way. Unfortunately, to try to keep the peace at home, we always gave in to him.

Daniel had started controlling everything we did, from the time we woke up in the morning, to when we slept at night. He insisted on putting Jessica to sleep at night and began watching her very closely. He watched her brush her teeth, both morning and night, and scrutinised her anytime she ate. He insisted on eating whenever she did and insisted on eating near her. He watched her every movement and became very agitated if Jessica dropped any food or had any food on her face. His eyes were very sharp, and even a crumb would be enough to cause him to have a meltdown. It got to the point that the only time Jessica could eat in peace was when Daniel was at respite.

At the dinner table, he objected to the glasses we were drinking from having fingerprints and marks from our mouths. He used a serviette to try to clean the marks off the glasses and became very agitated when he wasn't successful. We switched from glasses to plastic bottles, just to keep the peace.

Daniel also became concerned with the clothes Jessica and I wore. There was a variety of top that Jessica and I owned that he objected to. He also objected to stains on clothing, both his own and everyone else's. He changed his clothes numerous times a day and insisted that Jessica and I also change our clothes if they became stained at all.

Anytime we returned home, Daniel had to be the first person to go inside. He also had to go outside when anyone went outside or anytime he heard a plane. Sometimes, fed up with his own behaviour, he would just put one foot outside the door, instead of actually going out.

He began wanting to 'help' with everything. He wanted to vacuum, cook, water the garden and even put sugar on Simon's cereal. With his tendency to spill things, and his agitation over food and drink spills, there were a lot of tantrums. His need to be involved in everything made completing even the simplest of tasks both time-consuming and frustrating. As getting anything done while he was awake was difficult, it was tempting to try to get jobs done while he was sleeping. The problem with this was that he hardly slept. He slept when we slept at night and would often wake up extremely early. In spite of monitoring his sleep closely and not letting him sleep during the day, he still woke up any time after two a.m. To help him sleep, we gave him children's cough medicine in his apple juice. It didn't help. The early starts made for very long days that were extremely hard to fill.

As there was very little to amuse Daniel, he continued to seek his own stimulation. One of the ways he amused himself was by making noise. He wasn't just loud, he also moved constantly and continually checked on Simon, Jessica and me. He didn't sit still, and he was very seldom, if ever, quiet. He became obsessed with things such as Halloween, and spoke about it constantly. It was the same little loop that he repeated, and it drove everyone to the point of distraction. The loop started with him saying, 'What will happen? Knock at the door. Open the door, people say trick or treat.' This continued for months, and our favourite holiday fast lost all its appeal.

He also wanted the decorations for Halloween, birthdays and Christmas packed up and put away on the day. We accommodated his need to pack up promptly on birthdays and Halloween but tried to leave the Christmas tree up on Christmas Day. In the end, after Daniel repeating 'We put away' endlessly and becoming increasingly agitated, we gave in and packed up the Christmas tree and all other decorations on Christmas Day. Jessica didn't like it, but it was always Daniel's way.

Daniel's obsession with things wasn't restricted to Halloween. Anytime something out of the ordinary was going to happen, he had increased anxiety. He coped with his anxiety by continually mentioning the upcoming event. It got so frustrating that we avoided telling him about anything until we absolutely had to.

Daniel lashed out, and hit Jessica and me, anytime he had a tantrum. If we weren't close enough to hit, he threw things and tried to break things. He also hit himself, threw himself on the floor and scratched his own arms. He didn't like anyone, himself included, to have scratches or sores on their bodies. Any injuries he inflicted on himself would later cause him distress.

Daniel also objected to everyday tasks that needed doing. He objected to haircuts, getting his nails clipped and brushing his teeth. Another thing that caused major tantrums was anytime water was splashed on his face and, in particular, his eyes. Having water in his eyes was a major problem for him, so I always packed a face washer in his bag when he went swimming with the school. It didn't eliminate the tantrums, but hopefully it reduced their severity.

In November 2012, the bank where I was working wasn't going to tolerate my almost non-existent sales any longer. I was forced to resign and started the long, frustrating hunt for work.

At the end of the school year, Daniel's teacher told us about a concert that was held on the second last day of school. The concert finished at noon, with an afternoon tea to be shared by students, staff and parents. Following the afternoon tea, parents took their child home. The teacher also let us know that the last day of school was considered a cleaning day, and that most parents kept their children home from school. We sent Daniel to school on the second last day of school, with a plate of cupcakes, and picked him up at two-forty-five p.m. We also sent him to school on the last day and picked him up at the same time. Six weeks of school holidays were more than long enough for us, even if they weren't enough for his teacher.

Things were extremely difficult at home. We were once again trying to keep Daniel occupied during the holidays. Simon was still working night shift and sleeping during the day was virtually impossible, as Daniel never stopped making noise. Putting on a DVD didn't help, as when Daniel watched anything, he laughed loudly, sang along, danced and acted out whatever was happening on the screen. He turned a quiet, sedate activity into a noisy, high energy one. Anytime I asked him to be quiet, he laughed loudly and echoed the request in a very loud voice. It was frustrating for everyone, and Simon was exhausted to the point of collapsing. We also lost our beloved holiday program. The respite service stopped running the program, and so Daniel was at home, seven long days a week, for six long weeks.

The only relief we had was the three hours respite on a Saturday and the weekend stays. We looked forward to this so much that we counted the days and hours until respite. It was the only thing we looked forward to. If the support worker didn't show up on Saturday, we were all disappointed. When the respite service cancelled Daniel's weekend stay, due to a double booking, we were all devastated

I complained to Simon, 'It's always our weekend that gets cancelled. Why can't Oscar's respite get cancelled? He's not as bad as Daniel, and he's there every second weekend. It's not fair.'

'What do you want me to do about it? Simon replied, fed up and worn out. 'I can't do anything about it. I'm in the same leaky boat as you. I'm just not whingeing about it.'

He was right. There was nothing either of us could do about it.

Twelve

We survived the holidays, but when school was postponed for two days because of storm damage, we were devastated. It was the straw that broke the camel's back.

'I can't do this any more,' I told Simon. 'I really can't. I've had enough. We're not getting anywhere.'

'You're right. If we keep on going like this, one of us is going to end up breaking his arm or worse,' Simon said.

'Why are we even trying?' I asked. 'We don't get help from anyone. We've tried everything. Nothing has worked. Medication was useless, the intervention programs did nothing, and his behaviour just keeps getting worse.'

Simon nodded sadly and said, 'Are we even helping him by keeping him with us? Do you think he would be better off with another couple? People like Belinda and her husband. People who are positive and energetic, not too worn-out to even look after him, much less help him.'

'I don't know,' I said, 'but I know it's not fair on Jessica. She deserves to have a normal life, not this.'

Jessica loved to write, and often wrote short stories and poems. One day, she showed me a poem about Daniel. It was a beautiful, sad poem and the last line was particularly heartbreaking. It resonated with me and I still remember it all these years later. It read,

> He pulls my hair and pushes me into a shelf.
> Once again I am left crying by myself.

For a long time, we both felt that we couldn't cope. It felt like surrendering Daniel was inevitable. As he had become so much harder to handle, it was now not a matter of if, but when.

'I'll call Joan and I'll try to get respite for Daniel next weekend,' Simon said. 'I'll tell her it's an emergency and we can't cope any more.'

Daniel started a new school year, in a new class, with two new teachers. It was a relief just to have some peace and quiet again while he was at school. It was our sacred time, and probably the only thing that stopped us both having nervous breakdowns. Simon had successfully booked emergency respite for the weekend. So, on Friday, we dropped Daniel at school with no intention of picking him up on Monday.

All weekend, we thought over our options. On Monday, I made some phone calls. I called Disability Services, Child Safety and a free legal service. The information I received from the separate organisations was conflicting. Whereas one service seemed confident that Daniel would be placed in a foster home, another service was equally adamant that he would be placed in supported accommodation.

On Monday, we picked him up from school. Difficult as he was, and hard as he made life for everyone, we still couldn't give him up. He was still our little boy and we loved him dearly.

A week or so later, we had yet another meeting to discuss Daniel. An advocate for disabled people attended, as well as case managers from Disability Services Queensland and Evolve.

The advocate for the disabled looked at me with venom in her eyes and said, 'I'm only here for Daniel's sake. I'm not here for anyone else. I've no interest in helping you or your family, only Daniel.'

'If you help Daniel, we'll all benefit,' I replied, unimpressed by her rudeness and appalling attitude. 'By helping him, you'll also be helping our family, whether you intend to or not.'

'That's your opinion,' she replied angrily.

It was a common response any time I said anything that people didn't agree with. I didn't understand, and still don't understand, why they couldn't just say they didn't agree with me. I was, after all, completely aware that what I said was, for the most part, just my opinion. At no stage did I ever try to pass off my opinion as fact. It infuriated me as much as being told that we weren't a priority, and that they didn't have a silver bullet.

True to her word, the advocate for the disabled didn't do anything to help us as a family. She also didn't do anything to help Daniel. In fact, she didn't do anything.

While at the meeting, I complained that a number of reports about Daniel referred to his autism as moderate. I pointed out that his autism had never been diagnosed as moderate. I also pointed out, that although it wasn't in writing, a paediatrician at the hospital in 2007 confirmed that his autism was severe. A report, written by a member of the Evolve team on 14 October 2013 mentioned this point. It was typed as a footnote and was approximately half the size of the text in the rest of the report so could be very easily overlooked.

Another thing that was discussed at the meeting was accommodation for disabled adults. The case managers were reluctant to discuss the housing situation but eventually admitted that it cost taxpayers approximately 400,000 dollars a year to house one disabled adult. The case managers were reluctant to reveal the number or location of the houses used to accommodate disabled adults. Shortly after the meeting, we realised the house across the street from us was a house for disabled adults.

One of the case managers, who seemed more understanding than the others said, 'Look, I know you think no one understands. But I do. I've been in your boat. I know how hard it is. I have a disabled son. He's older than Daniel, and I had to surrender him when he was sixteen. I know what you're both going through, because I've been there myself.'

'I'm so sorry,' I said, surprised by his honesty and the fact that he was so forthcoming with personal information. 'I hope you don't mind me asking but how is your son now?'

'That's fine,' he said. 'I don't mind. My son's happy. In fact he's happier now living in supported accommodation than he was with me. I'm happier too. I'm not going to lie, though. It's been a struggle, and I only joined Disability Services Queensland because I thought I could make a difference.'

'Have you?' I asked.

'No. Not for lack of trying, but no, I haven't achieved anything,' he said, seeming defeated and completely depleted. 'It's almost impossible to implement even the smallest change, never mind any real improvement. I've given up even trying to change anything. The system is broken beyond repair. I only stay in the job so I can help my son. As I'm sure you are aware, when you have a disabled child, you have to fight for your child and your child's rights. You both have to be Daniel's advocates, otherwise your child will suffer.'

As is the norm in these types of meetings, funding – or more accurately, lack of funding – was mentioned.

'There simply isn't enough funding for disability,' one of the workers said.

'Actually,' I replied, 'there seems to be funding for everyone else, just not us. I know a woman, a customer from where I used to work. She got funding to have a pool built for her daughter. Now, on paper, she's worse off than us because she has two disabled children. In reality, she's much better off. Her children aren't anywhere near as bad as Daniel. She brings them to the bank and they behave. We can't take Daniel anywhere. How is that fair that we can't even get funding for respite but she can get a pool built? By the way, last time I saw her, she was complaining because she's struggling now with the cost of maintaining the pool. Not exactly money well spent.'

No one said anything and after a brief awkward silence, one of the representatives asked, 'What would you like?'

'More respite, a lot more respite,' I quickly answered.

'We'll see what we can do,' said the worker, making a short note.

As always, we were drained after the meeting, but completely aware that little if anything had been accomplished.

Realising that no one was going to help us, I tried to be more proactive in getting support. As Daniel had been diagnosed at the age of three and a half, I was keen to have him reassessed to know the severity of his autism. At one of Daniel's paediatric appointments, I asked if we could have him reassessed. The paediatrician told me that was something I needed to speak to the school about. The school said it was something that I needed to speak to the paediatrician about.

The school did organise for Daniel to be tested by a guidance counsellor, who conducted the equivalent of an IQ test and wrote a report. The report claimed he had the intellectual age of a four-year-old, and it did not measure in any way he severity of his autism. The end result was a report on his intelligence that I didn't agree with. After being given the runaround, I still didn't have an updated medical opinion on his autism. I gave up. Even if I was successful in getting a report recognising that his autism was severe, I suspected that there would always be other families in worse situations. I believed that we would always be considered low priority.

Even though we didn't go through with surrendering Daniel, the threat was enough to change the way Disability Services Queensland treated us. A new case manager was appointed, and we were also given funding, whereas previous funding requests had always been denied. The new case manager was efficient, hardworking and extremely patient and treated us both with respect. In a short time, the case manager successfully set up a National Disability Insurance Scheme (NDIS) plan for Daniel. The funding, however, was the only thing that changed. Daniel didn't receive any additional interventions, therapies or respite.

The hunt for work continued, and I sent resumés and letters of interest everywhere. As always, the rejection emails came in thick and fast. Eventually, I was successful in gaining part-time casual work as a sales assistant at a new manchester shop. The shop was scheduled to open in March 2013.

We muddled on. At the start of 2013, Simon decided to resign from his job. Working night shifts and dealing with Daniel were just too much for him, and he couldn't cope any longer. We were down to my just my part-time income. Our case manager at DSQ suggested we apply for a parenting payment, for parents with disabled children. Our application was approved and we started receiving a small fortnightly payment from Centrelink. It was significantly less than Simon's previous fortnightly earnings, and he continued to have anxiety about money.

With Simon not working night shift, things did improve a little.

Daniel's behaviour didn't improve, but at least Simon was able to sleep at night. Simon had greater energy, and we started taking Daniel out to more places. We began slowly, by taking him to supermarkets and hardware stores. We took him at night, when the stores were almost deserted, and the only people in the store were ourselves and staff. He became very agitated if anyone accidentally touched him or bumped into him. If that happened, he had to recreate the incident and bump that person back. To avoid confrontations and keep him calm, Simon and I walked with him in between us. Balloons were still a major issue, and there were many occasion when he refused to enter a store which was decorated with balloons.

As Daniel was now twelve and a half, both Simon and I were keen to try medication again. We were both hoping that as he was older and bigger, the paediatrician would be able to try a stronger medication to help with his anxiety. We believed his anxiety didn't just impede his quality of life. It was also impacting his ability to learn and reach his full potential. We went to our local GP, who was happy to give us a referral for a paediatrician at the local public hospital. Due to the severity of Daniel's anxiety and behavioural issues, the GP was kind enough to write that this was an urgent case, and Daniel needed to be seen as soon as possible. We took the referral to the hospital and started patiently waiting.

We mentioned to Daniel's two teachers that we were trying to get him an appointment with a paediatrician at the hospital. The teachers agreed that he would definitely benefit from medication for his anxiety. They wrote a letter explaining his anxiety and behavioural issues. They also recommended a public clinic for Indigenous Australians which saw patients regardless of ethnicity. We got a second referral from our GP. We took the teacher's letter to the hospital, and the new referral and letter to the clinic.

A year passed, and in spite of my numerous and frequent phone calls, we hadn't been given an appointment for a paediatrician at either the hospital or clinic. We got a new referral, as our original one had expired. We dropped the new referral at the hospital and clinic for Indigenous Australians. We didn't hear back from the clinic .

About a fortnight later, we received a letter advising that we had an appointment with a paediatrician at the hospital. The wait was finally over, and we were hopeful that we would at last get some help. We arrived at the hospital and waited with Daniel for our appointment. He was weighed and measured before we went in. The paediatrician was a young, inexperienced doctor who seemed unnerved by Daniel and his behaviour. He didn't throw tantrums while we were seeing the doctor but was his usual anxious self and couldn't sit still.

After brief introductions were made, the doctor asked, 'What is Daniel's diagnosis?'

'Autism, intellectual impairment, global delay, anxiety and severe constipation,' I replied.

'When was he diagnosed?' he asked.

'He was diagnosed in 2003,' I said. 'He was three and half years old. I've tried to have him reassessed since then, but I haven't gotten anywhere.'

'That isn't something that a paediatrician does. You need to see his school about that,' he responded.

Simon and I did what would we could to try to have Daniel sit quietly and behave, while we continued to answer questions. We weren't successful, and he caused havoc. He was increasingly getting on the doctor's nerves and wanted to touch everything in the small office. As he had developed a fascination with teeth, Daniel wanted my teeth examined. We tried to ignore his repeated requests and continued with the appointment. It became obvious that he wasn't going to settle until he had his way.

'Would you mind looking at my teeth?' I asked. 'It might appease him.'

The doctor looked disgusted, as if such a menial task was beneath him, but I opened my mouth anyway. I assumed that the paediatrician would only pretend to look at my teeth, just to humour Daniel.

He didn't pretend and didn't mince words either. 'You need to brush more,' he announced.

I was shocked by his rudeness but said nothing. We had waited over a year for this appointment, and now the paediatrician was a rude, arrogant pig of a man, who did nothing to hide his contempt for us.

We continued with the appointment and, after telling him about Daniel's anxiety and behavioural issues, asked for medication. We explained that we had previously tried behavioural interventions which didn't have any effect on his behaviour. We also explained that we had considered surrendering Daniel, and that Simon had given up his job so he could concentrate on him.

The paediatrician was unsympathetic and generally seemed uninterested in anything we had to say. We seemed to be taking up his valuable time, and it felt like he wanted to be anywhere but there.

'I can prescribe medication but it's by no means a silver bullet. It's very likely to have little or no effect,' he said.

We told him that we understood, and that we just desperately needed something that would take the edge off his anxiety and tantrums. We didn't expect a miracle cure, although we desperately needed it. We just wanted his behaviour to be more manageable and his tantrums less frequent and intense.

The paediatrician agreed to put Daniel on a very low dose of Risperidone, 1 mg per day. Risperidone is commonly used to treat anxiety and is often prescribed to autistic children to make them more manageable. In 2006, the Therapeutic Goods Administration approved Risperidone and Aripiprazole for the treatment of behavioural problems associated with autism spectrum disorder, in children as young as five. The starting dose of Risperidone is 0.25 mg per day in children weighing less than twenty kilos and 0.5 mg in people weighing more than twenty kilos. Depending on weight, doses may be increased by 0.25 mg to 0.5 mg at two-week intervals, with targets of 0.5 mg and 1 mg daily.

The doctor said, 'Give him half a tablet (0.5 mg) in the morning and half a tablet in the evening. If you don't notice any improvements after a week, increase the dose to one tablet (1 mg) in the morning and one tablet in the afternoon.'

We thanked him and were told that the time and date of Daniel's next appointment would be sent to our address. Given our previous experiences with medication, we were understandably sceptical about the strength of the new medication. It turned out there really wasn't any need to be.

We immediately took the script to the pharmacist and started the medication that night. A week passed and, as there wasn't any change in Daniel's behaviour or anxiety, we followed the paediatrician's instructions and increased his medication. The following afternoon, at about four p.m., he started leaning his head very slightly towards the left. It looked odd, but it didn't seem to be hurting him, and he was quite happy. We were, nonetheless, concerned and kept a close eye on him. It slowly and progressively got worse, until he seemed to be in pain and became quite worked up. We had no idea what was happening, but fearing he might be having a stroke, called an ambulance. Increased risk of strokes was one of the many possible side effects mentioned in the information about his new medication.

We had a very short wait and were relieved when the ambulance arrived. The officers were friendly, polite and professional. We explained our concerns regarding Daniel.

They greeted him warmly and briefly checked his vitals. 'How would you like to go for a ride in an ambulance?' they asked.

As he didn't respond, I answered for him. To help keep him calm, I rode in the back of the ambulance with him and the other ambulance officer, while Simon drove to the hospital.

Daniel seemed to be in pain and remained very agitated. I apologised to the officer, who was calm, relaxed and completely unbothered by his behaviour.

He assured me it was fine before turning his attention to Daniel. 'What do you like to play with?' he asked.

As Daniel didn't answer, I said, 'He likes balloons.'

'How about gloves?' the ambulance driver asked me.

'Gloves are good,' I replied.

The driver found a box of gloves and gave two to Daniel. Daniel was content for about thirty seconds.

'Would you like me to make you a rooster?' the officer asked after reassuring him.

'Yes, please,' I said, as Daniel didn't answer.

He made a rooster, all the while reassuring and praising him. 'What sound does a rooster make?' he asked, handing Daniel the rooster.

When Daniel didn't answer, he crowed like a rooster. He distracted him and kept him relatively calm for the entire drive to the hospital. His patience and energy seemed endless.

The ambulance drivers continued to look after him after we reached the hospital and were waiting to see a doctor. Simon and Jessica arrived shortly after the ambulance did. The drivers only left us when they received a call on their radio.

Even though it was a Wednesday night, and we lived in a small country town, the emergency department of the hospital was incredibly busy. As there were about eight patients waiting on stretchers to see doctors, Simon and I found a quiet unoccupied room in which to wait. Daniel, although in pain and extremely agitated, was still able to walk around. He had no interest in lying down and was noisy as always. The quiet room helped calm him and also stopped him from disturbing the other patients.

We waited a short time before we saw a doctor. The doctor went over the same questions as the ambulance drivers, and I answered their questions as accurately as possible. The diagnosis was that Daniel was having a dystonic reaction, as a result of being on too high a dosage of Risperidone. Simon and a couple of male nurses held Daniel, while the doctor administered the antidote in the form of an injection. The effect of the antidote was instantaneous, and he relaxed immediately. Simon and I were both extremely relieved and amazed at such an effective cure.

The doctors wanted to keep an eye on Daniel, just to make sure there were no other side effects from the Risperidone, or the amazingly strong antidote. They were happy for us to continue waiting in the small room that Simon and I laid claim to. Simon and I waited, while Jessica slept on a bed, and even Daniel seemed happy, calm and relaxed.

After waiting for about an hour, Daniel turned to me and said, 'Do a poo.'

We managed to find a bathroom just in the nick of time, and Daniel did his weekly poo at the hospital.

An hour or so later, the paediatrician came to check on Daniel, who was fine, so we were able to take him home. He was kind enough to write a letter explaining Daniel's reaction to his medication. He also advised us to reduce his dosage back to half a tablet in the morning and evening. We arrived home just before midnight. We sent Daniel to school the next day.

Thirteen

Over the following weeks, Daniel's behaviour improved, and his anxiety decreased. The medication had an amazing effect on his behaviour, and Simon and I were delighted. My anger eased and became less dominant. It happened gradually, and I was finally able to see families with normal children without seeing red.

The other effect of the medication was that Daniel suddenly had an appetite. He started asking for and eating food. As his speech was predominately echolalia, he asked for food by asking us if we would like food. For example, if he wanted spaghetti he would ask, 'Anyone want spaghetti?' He put on weight and went from underweight to a nice healthy weight. We gave him a new nickname, 'Spongy'.

One day after Daniel ate his lunch, we took him for a large chocolate sundae. His lunch was a generous serve of spaghetti and meatballs which he ate with gusto. When we arrived home, he sat at the kitchen bench and held his stomach. From the expression on his face, it might have been the first time in his childhood that he experienced feeling full. It was an odd, bizarre experience for him.

The ambulance drivers had been extremely patient with Daniel, and he developed a rapport with them in the short time that he spent with them. After his positive experience, anytime he became upset, he lay down on the floor and said, 'Call an ambulance.' It happened regularly, and Daniel requested an ambulance anytime Simon and I corrected him. We weren't too fussed by this new behaviour. We just hoped that he wouldn't do this at school or respite. We didn't want an overly anxious staff member or support worker calling an ambulance unnecessarily. Fortunately, it didn't happen.

With Daniel's improved behaviour and Simon's increased energy levels, we began taking Daniel out more, and for longer periods. We started taking him to coffee shops and took him during the day, instead of at the end of the day. We began doing more things as a family, and we all loved it. We started going shopping, eating in cafés, swimming at the local pool, going to the beach, and going on picnics. It was a relatively happy time for us. Daniel's vocabulary continued to increase, and he started communicating more at home, and at school.

Daniel also started wearing a jumper when we went out. The jumper was taken off, regardless of temperature, the second he got home. It was still progress, and both Simon and I were delighted. One item he still refused to wear was his school polo shirt. We mentioned it to his teachers, who assured us that as the polo shirt was not compulsory, it was not an issue. We didn't bother mentioning it to the occupational therapist or psychologist, as we assumed that we would only be told the reasons for not wearing the shirt. We had given up on anyone else resolving our issues with him.

Every year, Daniel's school took the students to the local show that was held in the next town. As he had been taken to the show the previous two years, we assumed that he would be taken this year. We signed the permission slip and returned it the following day in his communication book, with money in an envelope to cover the admission cost. On the day of the show, we ensured that we packed morning tea, lunch and a water bottle, as requested on the permission slip. As suggested, we included some spending money which could be used to either buy food or show bags. I also wrote down some food, as well as show bag suggestions, just to make things easier for the staff. We dropped him off at school that morning, happy that we had done everything that was mentioned in the permission slip. It was a cold morning, so most of the students were wearing jumpers. As there wasn't a school jumper, the students were all wearing a variety of brightly coloured jumpers.

About thirty minutes after we dropped him at school, Simon got a call from Daniel's teacher on his mobile phone. His teacher asked for a school polo shirt to be dropped off at the school, as he wasn't wearing one and didn't have one in his school bag. The teacher explained that it was a new school policy that all students had to be wearing the polo shirt anytime they were taken off the school grounds. Simon was fuming and told the teacher that he would be at the school in ten minutes to collect Daniel and take him home.

Less than a minute later, the same teacher phoned Simon again to tell him that she had found a spare school polo shirt in the office and was now about to help Daniel onto the bus. We continued with our day, and I crossed my fingers that Daniel was in a better mood than Simon. Later that week, we spoke to other parents and learnt that the show day was optional for students. The parents informed us that not all students went to the show, and that some stayed at school. Daniel's teacher hadn't mentioned any of that to Simon.

The following month, we had an appointment at the hospital with a different paediatrician. This time we had a lovely, caring doctor. We didn't make a complaint about the first paediatrician and, fortunately, we never saw him again.

Now that the shop I was working at had been open for more than six months, business slowed, and my hours were cut back to approximately fifteen hours a week. This caused more financial strain. Simon, who hadn't been unemployed since he was eighteen, missed working. He found work during the weekends as a driver for a medical organisation. Part of his job was to escort the doctor into the patient's house. One weekend, one of the appointments was for a severely disabled child who was non-verbal and lived with just the mum. After that night, Simon and I finally understood that there really were people worse off than us.

Another school year finished and with Daniel's behaviour significantly improved so we could go out; we didn't dread the holidays with the same passion as we had previously. From a very young age, Jessica was very good with Daniel. She was patient and always made an effort to play with him and amuse him. Even before she was a teen, she became the third adult in the family.

We changed Daniel's weekly respite to Saturday nights, as Simon and I were keen to start eating out at some of the local restaurants. One Saturday evening, the support worker was a little early, so Simon wasn't quite ready. She was new to the area and hadn't cared for Daniel before, so I introduced myself. We made small talk while Simon finished getting ready.

'Have you worked as a support worker for long?' I made the mistake of asking.

She didn't answer with the 'not long' or 'quite a while' answer I was expecting.

'I've been working in disability for almost twenty-five years,' she said. 'I started in 1987, and my first job was in a nursing home. I didn't mind that job but there were some high-needs young adults living there. I found that quite upsetting. So I left that after about five years, and I started work in a group home – twelve-hour shifts – and I'd look after three clients at once. I did both day shifts and night shifts. A lot of people prefer night shifts, but I actually prefer day shifts. It's more work, but at least it doesn't muck up your sleep pattern. I found working nights really hard. I was there for nearly ten years. After that, I found a job in Ozcare, and I looked after high-needs adults. I've peg fed, changed adult nappies, bathed and dressed adults. I loved that job, but I had to leave so I could be closer to my daughter. She had just had her first baby, so I wanted to help her. The only work I could find was in a nursing home. I really didn't enjoy working there, so I left after about two years. I found work with a respite service, and I also started working as a teacher aide at a special school. I loved that job but my husbands work transferred him here, so I had to leave. I actually much prefer working with children over adults. I love working with kids, they're so….'

'Sorry but have you met my husband, Simon and my daughter, Jessica?' I interrupted.

By that stage, Simon was ready and had joined us.

'Jessica's in the car,' he said, as I glanced around the living room. He then turned to the worker and said, 'Hi, I'm Simon. Nice to meet you.'

With Jessica already waiting in the car, we were able to make our exit and drove gratefully to the restaurant. We arrived home three hours later and, although Daniel seemed fine, the support worker looked worn out. We offered her a lift home, as she had been dropped off by her husband and didn't have a car with her. Daniel was still only having a bowel motion once a week and wasn't due to have one until Sunday. Just as we were about to hop in the car, Daniel stood perfectly still as a large poo dropped from his boxer shorts onto the garage floor.

Simon and I just laughed, and I quickly grabbed some gloves and tissues and picked up the poo. As I was doing so, I glanced at the support worker. She hadn't said a word and seemed to be in shock. In spite of her many years of extensive experience, she looked like a deer in headlights. We drove her home, and although we continued to have weekly respite for Daniel, we never saw her again.

Something that I wanted to try with Daniel for a long time was taking him to a movie. My parents had tried and failed in the past, and the school's previous attempts were not successful either. Even though I was well aware that the previous attempt to take him to the cinema had been summed up with 'We survived', I was still keen to try again. I wanted Daniel to start watching movies, as I thought going to the cinema was a great, relatively inexpensive way to kill time during holidays and weekends. At that stage, we hadn't been told about a companion card. This allowed a carer to receive a complimentary ticket. The companion card wasn't accepted everywhere but was accepted at a number of places, including the local cinema.

Daniel's improved behaviour, and his acceptance of sleeping with the lights off, gave us the confidence to try watching a movie at the cinema with him. It paid off, and the movie went well. We all enjoyed ourselves, and we had achieved something that, at one stage, I thought would never be possible. It was a proud, momentous occasion for all of us. We shared the news with my parents via text messages and accompanying photos. Real progress had been made at last.

As the movie was a success, we decided to try to take Daniel on a trip to Brisbane for a weekend. We were able to take him to the shops, a movie and to restaurants. Although he still had anxiety, he coped well with the crowds and noise of Brisbane. Feeling confident, we decided to take him on a plane. His first plane ride was to Brisbane, and he grinned from ear to ear for the entire flight. It was this progress that first planted the idea in Simon's mind that Daniel was able to cope with living in Sydney.

As Daniel's behaviour had become more manageable, we decided to stop respite. The relief we received from respite wasn't worth the anxiety and aggravation it caused. Although his behaviour and communication had improved, he still had severe anxiety about respite. He continued to repeat his annoying little loops about *Play School*, school, home and asking what we were having for dinner. We felt that we could cope without respite, and we would all be better off without it. We had finally come full circle, and both Simon and I were proud of ourselves. We couldn't have done it without the medication. In spite of the paediatrician's initial warning, the medication had done wonders and, as a result, our quality of life improved immensely.

Unfortunately, when we stopped respite, Daniel's anxiety didn't stop with it. He continued to mention respite for about eighteen months after we stopped having it. He didn't stop his mantras and loops so much as slowly reduce the number of times he repeated them. Gradually, he stopped. Now, four years later, we still don't ever say the word 'respite' as it still has the same consequences and causes just as much anxiety for him today. He also still continues to ask, 'What are we having for dinner?' He repeats the question many times throughout the day, and the repetition is indicative of both his anxiety and boredom.

Fourteen

At the end of 2014, we decided to move back to Sydney. We arrived in Sydney on 29 June 2015. We concentrated on enrolling the children in schools, finding full-time employment and an affordable rental. We enrolled Jessica at a local school without any difficulty but found it harder to enrol Daniel at a suitable school. Before he could be enrolled in a special school, we had to enrol him at a mainstream local high school. Once he wasn't accepted at the mainstream high school, we were able to enrol him at whichever special school was closest to our place of residence. When I complained and questioned the purpose of trying to enrol him in a mainstream school, I was told that this was the procedure. No other explanation was provided.

A special school which was a ten-minute walk away from my parents' house refused to accept Daniel, as it was already at maximum capacity. We were told he couldn't be enrolled there until 2016. We were finally successful at another school in a suburb that was twenty minutes away by train and a twenty-minute walk to the nearest train station.

Once we had successfully enrolled Daniel, we were advised that he wouldn't be able to start school until three weeks into the new term. The school claimed that the students in his class needed three weeks to get used to the idea of a new student. We weren't happy about the decision but reluctantly accepted it. His two-week holiday was extended to five weeks. Without the Internet to entertain him, it was a long and boring five weeks.

On his first day at his new school, Daniel dressed himself in his new uniform. He wore it with pride and was happy to be going back to school. The uniform was long navy slacks, a long-sleeved polo and a jumper. It was a big improvement from when he wouldn't wear long pants, jumpers, long-sleeved tops or even polo shirts. The three-week adjustment period for his new class didn't help, and he returned home from school with scratches on his arm. He was happy just to be back in a regular routine, and he soon settled into the new school.

Simon found part-time work on a contract basis. His hours were two to eight p.m. which was convenient, as it meant he could continue to take Daniel to school. Unfortunately, the new hours also gave him an excuse to revert to his tuna wraps diet. As I worked on a casual basis, I was able to reduce my hours so I could pick Daniel up from school of an afternoon.

Daniel seemed to cope well with travelling to and from his new school. The biggest challenge was coping with the noises of a typical Sydney suburb while we walked from his school to the train station. Sometimes he would be upset by the noise, while, on other occasions, he would feel the need to imitate the noises. Neither was a particularly good option, and I was always relieved when we arrived at the station. As his school finished at tw-forty-five p.m., the train and station weren't too crowded with children from other schools. There were still a number of noisy students on the train who grated on my nerves. Daniel, on the whole, coped with the noise and bustle of the train. He behaved well, but often repeated the announcements made on the train. He also insisted on saying, 'Bye train' when we got off at our station. We didn't apply for transport, as we were only staying with my parents on a temporary basis.

After three long months of living with my parents, we moved into a two-bedroom unit. On Monday 21 September 2015, Simon started a new full-time job, and I attempted to unpack and turn a two-bedroom unit into a functioning home for four people and a dog. It was also the first day of school holidays and the first time I took Daniel out by myself.

We walked to the shops, and I took him straight to Donut King for some donuts and a drink. After he devoured his food, I started walking with him towards the supermarket. We had only taken a few steps when

Daniel took off running. I caught up to him and found him standing at the top of an escalator. My nerves were shot, but I was very relieved to have caught up to him. He had spotted one of his teachers from his school and, being sociable, wanted to say hello. The teacher noticed him and started walking up the escalator that was going down. She stumbled but recovered her balance and made it to the top. It all happened too fast for me to react. If I had my wits about me, I would have taken Daniel on the escalator, which would have been the safer option. Luckily, his teacher wasn't hurt and after introductions and a brief chat, we continued to the supermarket.

While at the supermarket, I noticed a toddler playing up while shopping with his mother. Daniel, of course, also noticed the boy and was amused by both the child's misbehaviour and the mother's annoyance.

His mother, frustrated and fed up, turned to her son and asked, 'Do you want a smack?'

Daniel, not to be left out, joined in and loudly said, 'I'm going to give you a nack,' meaning a smack.

The little boy, obviously wanting a snack, looked up hopefully. I quickly and quietly led Daniel into another aisle before he had the chance to smack the boy. I hastily apologised to the boy's mother, who seemed too worn out to even care.

By the time we finished shopping, my nerves were so frazzled that I left the supermarket without paying for my shopping.

I didn't realise until after the cashier said, 'Excuse me, but you haven't paid for your shopping.'

In spite of my misadventures, I took Daniel shopping every morning. Shopping was a good way to get him out of the unit and establish some sort of routine for him. Spending time alone with him increased my confidence, and I began to relax a little. One of the things I noticed about Daniel was his fondness for police. Whenever we walked past a police officer, he waved and said, 'Hello, police', approximately five centimetres from their face. His school had successfully taught Daniel that the police are his friends and to say 'hello' to his friends. His school, unfortunately, was less successful in teaching him about volume control and personal space. While some police officers looked decidedly uncomfortable, most were friendly and polite. With time, my embarrassment diminished as more and more local police got to know Daniel and me. I joked with my parents that I had become 'known to the police'.

Although the police were friendly and accepting, other people unfortunately weren't. One day, Daniel and I were waiting to cross at a particularly busy intersection. We had pressed the button for the lights and were both just quietly waiting. I noticed another lady at the crossing and was surprised by her nervous manner. She looked at Daniel and then began frantically pressing the button. It took me a couple of seconds to realise that she was genuinely scared of him. I knew that in some cultures disabled people are believed to be possessed by the devil. I just didn't expect anyone in Australia to believe it. I felt bad for the lady, so to try to put her mind at ease, I made a feeble attempt at small talk and remarked on the lovely weather we had been having. It didn't help, and she continued to look at Daniel nervously. When the light finally turned green, we were both extremely relieved. The lady hastily crossed the road, eager to put as much distance as possible between us.

It wasn't an isolated case, and I noticed that, while shopping, Daniel and I were given a wide berth. People tended to stay clear of us, in much the same way as they steer clear of intoxicated or mentally disturbed people. They also tended to stare, regardless of Daniel's behaviour. One day, while waiting to be served at Donut King, I noticed a father and his young daughter standing away from the shop. The father carried his daughter while continually glancing over at us. As soon as we were served and left the counter, the father went to the counter to place an order.

The holidays flew by and, with a lot of effort, I got much of the unpacking done. When the children returned to school, the unpacking accelerated, and I was able to get a lot more done in a day. Slowly but surely, the chaos gave way to order. After a month, the unit was tidy, organised and as homely as possible. Due to the unit's proximity to the school, I was able to walk Daniel to and from school every day. It gave me a real sense of empowerment, and it was a huge relief not having to rely on someone else to take him to and from school.

I picked up Daniel from school every day at two-forty-five p.m. and, although he loved school, he was always happy to walk home with me. One afternoon, I noticed that he seemed very tired. He constantly put his head on my shoulder while we were walking. I thought it was very sweet and endearing, but didn't think too much of it.

About halfway to our unit, Daniel said, 'Lie down.' He repeated it several times and became increasingly anxious.

I reassured him that we didn't have far to go, and we kept walking.

He then said, 'Do a poo! Do a poo! Do a poo! Do a poo!'

He became very distressed, so I took him to a preschool that was on the way to our unit. I knocked on the door and asked if my son could use the bathroom. I explained the situation to the lady who answered. She let us into the preschool. Before I had a chance to react, Daniel rushed into the students' bathroom. As he was already sitting on a toilet and had started his bowel movement, I didn't have any choice but to close the door and let him finish. I hastily had him wipe his bottom, so I could flush the toilet. To my relief, one flush managed to clear a week's worth of poo. We washed our hands and went to leave.

Before we had a chance to discreetly leave, the preschool director approached us with a purposeful stride and an angry expression on her face. I don't know if she hadn't realised that Daniel was disabled or simply didn't care.

'Excuse me, but this is not at all appropriate,' she said. 'I have young children here that are impressionable and need to be protected. I have parents that are going to be arriving at any minute to pick up their children. They can't see this sort of thing happening.'

I was so happy and relieved that Daniel had his bowel movement, it was all I could do not to stand there and grin like a village idiot. I must have looked contrite enough, because the second her rant was finished, she took a completely different approach. Before I had a chance to speak, she sighed and continued in a softer tone.

'Look, if your son needs to use the bathroom again, can you please just take him to the staff bathroom at the back. Your son needs to have privacy.'

'You're completely right,' I said. 'I'm sorry. It won't happen again.'

By some small miracle, Daniel had stood still and remained silent during our brief conversation. To everyone's relief, it turned out to be an isolated incident.

After that incident, anytime I collected Daniel from school, I discreetly asked him if he needed to use the bathroom before we left. It didn't always help.

On another afternoon while walking home, Daniel calmly said, 'Lie down.' He was calm and relaxed, and when he rested his head on my shoulder I assumed he was tired. He remained calm but kept repeating, 'Lie down, lie down, lie down.'

We passed the preschool and were only about five hundred metres from home, when Daniel said, 'Do a poo.'

I didn't want to go back to the preschool, as it was roughly the same distance to our unit. We pressed on, and Daniel started to become anxious.

He repeated, 'Do a poo. Do a poo. Do a poo. Do a poo. Do a poo. Do a poo.'

We kept walking. I comforted and encouraged him as his anxiety continued to escalate. About three hundred metres from home, he stopped walking and stood perfectly still. I watched in horror as a large poo dropped from his shorts onto the pavement. It was a busy road, but fortunately, although there was plenty of traffic, we were the only people on the street. We left the poo on the street and hurried home.

Once at home, Daniel did the rest of his bowel movement in the toilet. I cleaned him up and ran a bath for him. Once he was happy in the bath, I grabbed a poo bag and collected the poo from the street. Luckily, the street was still empty, and no one had stepped in it. After that, I carried a roll of Penny's poo bags in my handbag. Fortunately, I never needed them, and that incident was also an isolated one.

With the unit unpacked and the children at school, my first priority was finding a paediatrician for Daniel. I checked with his new school and was told that it didn't have a paediatrician who held clinics there. I was sceptical but accepted that I would have to find him a paediatrician outside of school. I spoke to a GP and was given a referral for a medical centre for intellectually disabled people. I rang the clinic and was pleasantly surprised to be told that a patient had just cancelled. There was an appointment next week which I gratefully accepted.

Getting to the clinic involved catching a bus and train as it was in a suburb that didn't have a train station. It took approximately an hour to get there. The paediatrician was a lovely polite lady, and both Daniel and I warmed to her immediately. The usual introductions were made, and the paediatrician set about getting Daniel's medical history.

'When was Daniel diagnosed?' she asked.

'We had him assessed in Sydney on 3 December 2003, because we were concerned that he wasn't speaking,' I replied. 'He had other developmental issues, but the main one was his lack of speech and social skills. He was diagnosed with autism and a global developmental delay.'

She nodded and asked, 'So is that when you said, what do we do now?'

'Not quite,' I replied, dumbfounded.

It wasn't the first time a professional had given me that response, but I was still shocked. The first time was when I was volunteering as a teacher aide at Jessica's school. One of the teachers said the same exact thing when I told her about getting Daniel's diagnosis. I was so surprised that I just mumbled a quick, 'Not quite', before steering the conversation in another direction.

I was surprised, as both women were professional, intelligent and very compassionate. It just proved how little people understood the impact that learning that your child has a permanent disability has on parents. Of course, my response didn't help any.

She paused and after realising that I wasn't going to elaborate, asked, 'So how did you get here? Did you drive? Did you have any problems finding us?'

'I don't have a driver's licence,' I replied. 'We caught a train and then a bus.'

She seemed surprised and asked, 'Why didn't you make an appointment at his school?'

'I called his school and spoke to one of the ladies at the office, and she was adamant there wasn't a clinic at the school,' I replied.

She seemed bewildered but assured me that there was, and we made a second appointment for six months' time.

With Daniel back at school, I was able to work during the week, as well as weekends. As Simon was working full-time, I was responsible for taking Daniel to school and picking him up. It meant I was only able to work from ten a.m. to one p.m. After school, Daniel was content to either play on his iPad, watch me cook, or watch the clothes dryer. He also liked to snack on canned whipped cream which he referred to as 'shaving cream'. He was often very content to eat his 'shaving cream' from a bowl with a spoon while watching the clothes dryer. When we lived in a house, we didn't have a dryer, so it was a novelty for him. Simon put a stereo in the kitchen, which, although small, was gallery style, so there was a small area where he danced.

As Simon was at work, and Jessica spent time with her friends, it was often just the two of us in the unit. Daniel seemed to like the time we spent together, and we bonded well during our time in Sydney. It was the first time since his diagnosis that I felt the same love for him that I felt before his diagnosis. It happened gradually, and I was barely aware of it at the time.

Simon continued with his tuna wrap diet. Initially, he promised he would start eating once we moved into a place of our own. After we moved, he changed his mind, and said once he had completed the training. The five-week training period passed, and then he decided that he would start eating again once he was made permanent. It felt like he was never going to eat normally. He constantly told me, 'I don't know how to eat.' It was both heartbreaking and frustrating. He didn't know how to eat, and I didn't know how to help him. We plodded on.

He eventually started eating with us in the evening but insisted on eating only dinner, and only a child's serve. He would also occasionally binge on food. The bingeing didn't have the same effect as the first time, and he would usually feel angry and depressed after he ate. He was frustrated that I wasn't helping him with his eating disorder when he so desperately needed help. He wanted me to take him to the hospital, but I refused. I was convinced that the hospital wouldn't help, and the only thing that would come of it was a permanent history of mental illness on his record. I didn't want to do anything to make things worse, so regrettably I didn't do anything.

Fifteen

We all settled well into the unit. It was cramped but bearable. There were a lot of little things that we needed to get used to. The kitchen was much smaller, the front door couldn't be deadlocked, and the bathrooms and bath were also much smaller. The unit had a large balcony which was soon filled with portable clothes lines, and a small area that was covered with stones. That was where Penny went to the bathroom.

One day, after Penny did a poo, Daniel pointed to it and asked hopefully, 'Daniel step in the poo?' When he started walking toward the poo, I knew that he still was seeking sensory input. Although his 'poo painting' days were behind us, I knew he would still play with poo if the opportunity ever arose.

Although his language and behaviour had improved, Daniel was still scared of balloons and still incredibly sensitive to loud noises. There was a school across the road from my building. It had a sports carnival that was still going one day when I picked him up. We were about five hundred metres from home when he heard the first starter gun. He immediately started trying to run. I held firmly onto his hand and tried to reassure him. The gun continued to be fired at very short intervals. He became increasingly agitated and started running. I held his hand and ran with him for about two hundred and fifty metres. It is a fairly steep hill, and although I am not at all fit, he is surprisingly very fit. I stopped running, as I was completely out of breath. I let go of his hand.

Still very anxious, Daniel used this opportunity to take off. He didn't run very fast, and I watched him run ahead of me as I jogged behind him, trying to catch up. I saw him stop at our block of units. I reached our block, expecting to see him, but, to my absolute horror, I only saw a man collecting his mail. My stomach sank, and I was instantly filled with dread as my mind was flooded with worst case scenarios. We lived in a security building, so the only way to enter was with a key.

'Did you see a boy in a red polo shirt?' I asked.

'He went into the building with another guy,' he said. 'They walked in together, so I assumed they were together.'

I thanked him, let myself in and found Daniel waiting quietly at our front door. I was immensely relieved. It was not the only occasion when disaster was narrowly avoided.

Although I regularly ran baths for Daniel, I still wasn't completely used to the much smaller bath that we had in the unit. I put him in a bath one night and, while it was filling, tried to tidy up in the kitchen. I completely forgot about the bath and concentrated on cleaning up. Jessica and Simon were watching TV, and everyone seemed to be in good spirits. I heard Daniel start to whinge and went to see what was wrong. The tap was still on, and the bath was overflowing onto the bathroom tiles. There was about an inch of water on the bathroom floor, and it was seconds away from leaking onto the carpet. Without saying a word, I turned off the tap and frantically mopped the bathroom floor. Daniel hopped out of the bath shortly after I finished mopping. Simon and Jessica remained completely unaware that I had almost flooded the unit.

On another occasion, Penny vomited on Jessica's bed. As putting new sheets on the bed was challenging enough in the small space, I closed Jessica's bedroom door. Daniel has a tendency to shadow me, and Penny tends to lie on the beds anytime I make them up. Jessica was in her room at her desk, and I assumed that Simon and Daniel were watching TV in the living room. After I changed the sheets, I opened the door to Jessica's room. Jessica and I were going to join the others and watch some TV before turning in for the night. When I opened Jessica's door, I saw Daniel walk in through the front door. We were all stunned. No one had heard him leave, and we had assumed he was in the unit. We didn't ask him when he left, or where he went, as he wouldn't have been able to answer. Unfortunately, although Daniel's speech had progressed, he was mostly unable to answer questions. I assumed he went outside looking for me. Where he went, and how long he was outside, remains a mystery.

Daniel was very happy at school and had adjusted really well to living in Sydney. I was coping well with him and feeling relatively positive. Everything was going smoothly, until I had a meeting at his school to discuss post-school options. As he was only in year ten and still had two more years of school, I hadn't given much thought to post-school activities. I was completely unprepared, and the meeting didn't go well. In spite of being bombarded with information, at the end of the meeting I still didn't know what post-school activities were available. The only thing I learnt was that Daniel was too disabled to work, but not disabled enough to be in the sort of program that would benefit him most.

Daniel was taught by two teachers that year. Judy taught on Monday and Tuesday, while Gayle taught his class Wednesday, Thursday and Friday. Both of them, and a third lady whose job title and purpose was unclear, were at the meeting. As the meeting was scheduled for eight-thirty a.m. and the school opened at eight-thirty-five, Daniel joined us for the first five minutes. We all took our seats.

'Ruby, this is Liz and her son Daniel,' Gayle began. 'Liz, this is Ruby, who knows everything about disability and is a great source of information.'

'Daniel is a very placid child,' Ruby confidently stated.

We had not even been there for a minute, and Daniel was sitting quietly, which in itself was unusual behaviour. Dumbfounded, no one said a word until I broke the silence.

'No. He isn't. He really isn't,' I said shaking my head.

Ruby rolled her eyes and glared at me with utter contempt.

A staff member walked Daniel to the playground, and I wished I could join them.

'Daniel had a really good time at camp,' Gayle said, trying to ease the tension.

'That's great. How did he behave?' I asked.

'There were a few occasions when he got very upset,' she said. 'He had a few meltdowns and tantrums.'

'What do you mean by having a tantrum?' Ruby asked. 'What does he do when he's agitated?'

'Would you like a demonstration?' I asked, bemused. 'I can show you exactly what he does.'

'No, that won't be necessary,' she replied, unamused and unimpressed.

The meeting went from bad to worse, at a nice steady pace. Ruby bombarded me with information, none of which was particularly useful in our situation. She handed me several pieces of paper and continued to pass me information sheets and pamphlets throughout the meeting. By the end of the meeting, I had accumulated a mountain of reading material. She spoke at length about taxi subsidies, parking permits, school transport and respite. She also mentioned Centrelink payments for mobility equipment and adult nappies.

'What preparations have you made for when Daniel finishes school?' Ruby asked.

'I haven't done anything,' I answered honestly. 'He's only in year ten. He'll still be at school for another three years.'

'You can't wait three years,' she retorted in disgust. 'You need to get Daniel into programs now, not in three years' time. No one is going to do this for you.'

'But if I get him into a program now, he might be sick of it by the time he finishes school,' I argued.

Fed up, she shook her head and sighed, 'There is a disability expo that you really need to attend. I wouldn't recommend that you go by yourself. It can be quite overwhelming. Even clued-in people struggle with it,' she said. 'Have you at least started the paperwork so Daniel can get a pension when he turns sixteen?'

'No, I called Centrelink and was told that I can only do the paperwork after he turns sixteen.'

'That information is incorrect,' she said.

We were fifty-five minutes into a meeting that had been scheduled for an hour. Amongst other topics, we had discussed Daniel, his behaviour, and respite, but I still had no idea what options were available for him when he finished school.

'What you would like for Daniel?' Judy finally asked.

'Ideally, I would love him to be in a program that runs from nine a.m. to three p.m. Monday to Friday. I would want him to be in a small group, maybe five or six children. I think that will keep him in a good routine and keep him stimulated.' I then added, 'Routine is extremely important, and he gets bored a lot. I also want him to socialise with people his own age.'

'That is never going to happen,' she said, shaking her head, unwilling to sugar coat words.

I stared in disbelief, and she continued.

'It could happen if Daniel was able to work unsupported in one of the work places for the disabled. He is never going to be able to work unsupported. There are post-school placements available Monday to Friday, from nine to three. – unfortunately, they are only available to people who are more disabled and need more support than him.'

'So where does that leave Daniel?' I asked.

She just shrugged in response.

'I think we should wrap this meeting up,' Gayle said, as we had gone over the allotted time. 'Thank you for coming in today.'

'That's fine,' I said, 'I wasn't working today.'

Ruby seemed surprised and said, 'I didn't know you worked. Where do you work?'

'I'm a casual at Pillow Talk,' I replied.

'What's Pillow Talk?' she asked, looking puzzled.

'It's a manchester shop,' Gayle said. 'It sells bed linen, towels and so on.'

'Oh, I thought you were a sex worker,' Ruby said, seeming disappointed. An awkward silence followed before she lamely added, 'Because of the name.'

Frustrated and fed up, I wanted to yell, 'Do I look like a f#cking sex worker?' Instead, I shook my head. 'No, I'm not a sex worker.'

After the meeting, my moral nosedived. I felt disheartened and pessimistic, and grumbled my way through the days and weeks. I foolishly took Ruby's advice and applied to Centrelink for a pension before Daniel turned sixteen. It caused confusion and the procedure took three times as long as it should have. I was relieved when it was approved. I also got Daniel to start wearing underwear. It was something that was discussed in the meeting and was long overdue. I used balloons as an incentive. Every day after school, I gave Daniel balloons. He blew them up and twisted them so they resembled grapes. He then had a bath and would pop all the balloons in the bath. It became a daily routine which lasted about six months.

Fortunately, I met a lovely friend, who lived in the block of units next to mine and had a son at Daniel's school. My friend had an intellectual impairment and was a single mother to a young boy who was confined to a wheelchair and also has an intellectual impairment. Both my friend and her son suffered from various health issues. In spite of it all, she was always happy and volunteered in the community on a regular basis. She was never without a smile on her face, and she never failed to put one on mine.

Work was also a welcome distraction and keeping busy helped. I continued to try to find more work closer to home but, in spite of my efforts, was unsuccessful. My very limited availability was the biggest issue. I put Daniel's leaving school out of my mind, and my mood gradually brightened. Although I could cope with him, there were still days when his behaviour was extremely challenging. Some days were a nightmare, and his tantrums were intense and never ending.

Immediately after Daniel was diagnosed in 2003, I stopped immunising Jessica. At the end of January 2016, I received a letter from Centrelink stating that all children were now to be immunised. In order to keep receiving child care payments, I had to comply and have Jessica immunised.

When Simon saw the letter, he turned to me and said, 'You're the one who didn't want to get her immunised, you deal with it.'

As Jessica was only thirteen, I had to take both her and Daniel to the medical centre. As she required several vaccinations, I had several appointments. They involved lengthy waiting periods which Daniel didn't cope with. He was highly agitated and loud, and continually tried to hit Jessica. Although he didn't have a full-blown tantrum, he was disruptive enough that we attracted stares from the other patients in the full waiting room. He remained anxious while we saw the doctor, and even though the appointments only lasted fifteen minutes, it was long enough to leave the doctor frazzled.

As Daniel loves the *Wiggles*, I was keen to take him to their concert. He had previously been to a *Wiggles* concert ten years earlier with his school. Although he didn't enjoy it, I was keen to try again, as he had progressed a lot in the last ten years. I found seats for us at the back of the hall. We were close to both the exit and bathrooms. he had been fed, and I had taken him to the bathroom. He seemed in good spirits, so I started to relax a little. A minute later, a child carrying a sword-shaped balloon entered the room. Daniel immediately started crying and became very agitated. He was still very scared of balloons if he didn't have control of them.

'We put the balloon away,' he said. 'We put the balloon away. We put the balloon away. We put the balloon away.'

I did everything I could to try to calm him down. I motioned him to be quiet by putting a finger to my lips. I tried to comfort him, and I tried to distract him. Nothing worked. He remained extremely anxious and agitated, and the child who had the balloon had disappeared somewhere into the audience. Another child carrying a pink balloon walked into the room. Daniel was on the verge of having a major tantrum, and nothing I did seemed to help at all. I was at my wits end and completely out of ideas.

I did the only thing I could. I told Daniel to stay in his seat, and I approached the child's father. They were only a few seats in front of us, so I could still see Daniel looking very agitated in his seat.

'Hi, um, my son is autistic, and he's actually very upset by your daughter's balloon. That's him,' I said, pointing to Daniel. 'Do you think it's possible that I could give the balloon to him? It would help so much, and I would really appreciate it. I wouldn't ask if I wasn't desperate.'

'It's really not up to me,' he replied, unmoved by my plight. 'It's up to my daughter. You'll have to ask her.'

I turned to his daughter, 'My son is very sad because he wants your balloon. Do you think I can give it to him?'

The little girl nodded solemnly and handed me the balloon.

'Thank you so much, sweetheart,' I said, extremely relieved and grateful. 'You are such a lovely girl. Thank you so much, you are so kind.'

I returned to Daniel, who remained anxious and worked up.

'We put the sword away. We put the sword away. We put the sword away. We put the sword away,' he said.

I had no idea where the child with the sword balloon was, but I knew that Daniel wasn't going to calm down until he had it. This time I took him with me, as I knew he was much more likely to spot the sword than I was.

I found the child and approached his mother. 'Excuse me,' I said. 'I don't mean to disturb you but…'

The boy's mother took one look at Daniel and handed me the balloon. 'There you go. I wouldn't give this balloon to a normal child. I'm only giving it to you because your son is autistic.'

'Thank you,' I said, grateful and surprised that I didn't need to explain.

Worn out, I took Daniel and the two balloons to the nearest bin. We disposed of them and returned quickly to our seats. Daniel had calmed down but was still anxious. I was at the end of my tether and hoped against hope that there wouldn't be any more balloons or meltdowns.

Once the concert started, Daniel was happy and danced and sang very loudly. Occasionally, other mums turned to look at him, but on the whole, they were more interested in taking selfies.

When the concert was over, Daniel and I were the first people out the door. He remained anxious, even after we arrived home. He alternated between throwing tantrums and sobbing like his heart was broken. I alternated between correcting him and comforting him. It was a long, miserable afternoon.

Even though taking Daniel out was difficult and often left me frazzled, I persisted, as staying home wasn't a viable option. He still threw tantrums in public and at times, needed to be restrained. He seemed to enjoy watching movies, so I took him to the cinema fairly regularly. Before the movie began, He would laugh, echo the advertisements and sing. Although he was quite boisterous before it started, he was usually quiet during the movie. He also had a tendency to stand up and put his hands in the air before the movie began. To minimise the disruption to other patrons, we sat away from other people at the back of the cinema.

Sixteen

The weeks passed at a steady pace. After many months of looking, we bought a two-bedroom unit that seemed suitable. It took about a month to unpack, and even less time for the reality of living in a two-bedroom unit to really sink in. Weekends were particularly bad.

Everything about living in the unit was inconvenient. There wasn't a linen cupboard, so my linen was housed in four large plastic boxes which were placed in the built-in wardrobe in the master bedroom. I had pared down my linen cupboard to just essentials, but as Daniel still wet the bed, I needed a number of waterproof mattress protectors. Due to his fear of storms, he had a tendency to wet the bed when it rained. The mattress protectors couldn't be dried in the dryer, so I resorted to drying them in front of the heater. The stench from Daniel's bed filled the unit and lasted all day.

We applied for transport for Daniel and were successful. He was picked up outside the unit between eight and eight-ten every school morning. While waiting, he imitated any noises from birds, traffic and machinery that he heard. I was always appreciative of quiet mornings but, unfortunately, there always seemed to be noise. The transport proved incredibly reliable and I was relieved, as well as pleasantly surprised.

Although Daniel was relatively well behaved at home, school was another matter. Every afternoon, I read his communication book with a sense of dread. More often than not, there was an incident report or a message advising that he had either hit someone or had some sort of meltdown.

While the children were at school, I worked whenever I was able to. The dreaded communication book was still filled with incident reports. Daniel's teachers requested a meeting with me to discuss his behaviour and to come up with strategies to deal with it. Foolishly, I didn't make an appointment, as I felt that I didn't have any strategies or solutions for his behaviour.

The second school term finished, and with Daniel and Jessica on holidays, my work was cut back to weekends only. I settled into a regular holiday routine which involved taking Daniel for breakfast, followed by shopping. He still played up from time to time, but was usually relatively well behaved. The mid-year, two-week holidays passed without incident.

Taking Daniel out made the holidays pass a lot quicker, but he was still always happy to return to school. For me, school holidays were an unnecessary reminder of what the future held when he finished school. In spite of his progress, the end of his schooling still loomed over my head, like a huge black cloud of misery and despair. I dreaded the end of his schooling the way I used to dread school holidays.

A week after he started back at school, the principal called to advise me that Daniel had been suspended for possibly up to three weeks. He had pulled his teacher's hair. Unfortunately, he had caught her completely off guard and managed to pull her to the floor. I pleaded with the principal and asked if there was any way she would reconsider the suspension. The principal stayed firm, and we scheduled a meeting on Thursday at the school to discuss his suspension.

As expected, Simon didn't take the news well, and we spent most of the evening arguing. It was the usual argument of blaming each other that revolved in a never ending cycle of frustration.

'This is all your fault,' he said. 'You spoil him and mother him too much. I'm working. I can't deal with this. You need to sort it out.'

We didn't resolve anything, and it was left to me to deal with the suspension. It was another great start to the weekend. I appealed against the suspension, on the basis that Daniel couldn't control his behaviour. My appeal was unsuccessful and the suspension remained. To try to help resolve his behavioural issues, I made an appointment with his paediatrician. She suggested we try increasing his medication, and that he start taking medication at lunchtime.

Daniel's teachers, the principal, and a guidance counsellor were present at the meeting.

As soon as we sat down, I turned to his teacher and said, 'I'm very sorry Daniel pulled your hair. He's very sorry too, and if he could, he would tell you that. He likes you a lot.'

'No need to apologise,' his teacher graciously replied. 'He didn't mean to do it. I'm very fond of Daniel too, and I love having him in my class. He really is a lovely boy.'

'Moving forward,' the principal said, 'does anyone have any suggestions as to how to help Daniel cope at school?'

'I had an appointment with his pediatrician and she has recommended that he starts taking half a tablet of Risperidone at lunch times. She thinks it will take the edge off his anxiety and just help him cope better.'

Everyone was agreeable to Daniel taking medication.

'That sounds great,' the principal said. 'I'll get you to fill in the paperwork at the office once the meeting is finished. Of course you'll need to bring the medication to school in Webster packaging. Are there any other suggestions?' she added.

'I think you should only speak to him when you need to. He doesn't really like a lot of talking, and he just doesn't cope well with it. At home, I only speak to him if I have to.'

'If you are agreeable, I think we should try a behavioural intervention,' one of Daniel's teachers added, turning to me. 'I think we should try Sunnyfield Disability Service.'

'That's fine with me,' I readily agreed.

'That's sounds great,' the principal decided. 'Does anyone have anything else to add?'

We all shook our heads.

'Well, thank you all for coming today. I'm happy for Daniel to return to school on Tuesday,' the principal concluded.

I was ecstatic and relieved that the meeting had gone well. I took Daniel home, glad that I had good news for Simon.

Sunnyfield Disability Services is a group of behavioural therapists, and the school organised a referral later that day. As Daniel was in year eleven and had been suspended as a result of his behaviour, I was assured that his case would be treated as a priority. A few days after the meeting, I received a letter confirming his referral had been accepted and that he had been placed on their allocations register. I waited a couple of months before calling Sunnyfield Disability Services. I was assured that he was still on the waiting list. I called a second time three months later and a third time and was told the same thing. In spite of my phone calls, I didn't ever hear back from Sunnyfield Disability Services.

Daniel was happy to be back at school and the medication at lunchtime seemed to improve his behaviour significantly. His school situation had improved, but things remained miserable on the home front.

'Wow, you're home late,' I said to Simon one evening.

'That's because I hate coming home to this unit, and I hate coming home to you,' Simon snapped, tired, hungry and irritable.

I was by now so accustomed to his harsh tone and bitter words that his statement left me cold and indifferent. It was a stark contrast to happier times in our marriage when Daniel was a baby, and we were both happy when Simon came home. I remembered a time when Simon frequently said, 'This is my happy time. I'm home with my beautiful wife and beautiful boy.'

His anger and cruel words just confirmed what I had suspected. I felt the same way and also went to work early and delayed going home whenever I could. It was only about nine months after we had bought the unit, but we already felt that we couldn't live there any longer.

We discussed moving. Many of our discussions disintegrated into blaming one another and name calling. Arguing was still, unfortunately, a common method of communication for Simon and me. These days, our arguments lasted longer and were often followed by days of stony silence and tension. We eventually decided that we would move to Brisbane. Simon's energy levels and morale continued to plummet, while his anxiety and depression spiralled out of control. He spent the majority of his weekends in bed, and after he resigned from his beloved job, spent nearly all of his time in bed.

    To try to help Simon, I started doing the grocery shopping before work. When a cashier asked me if I had just finished nightshift, I was reminded that I wasn't hiding my exhaustion as well as I would have liked. After we sold our unit, Simon started to eat a little more. The extra food increased his energy, and the promise of a new start gave his morale a much needed boost. In good spirits and with high hopes, we moved to Brisbane at the end of June 2017.

Epilogue

Simon has settled into his job and is happier than he has been for a long time. Jessica is well-established in her school and has made a lovely group of friends. Daniel has also settled into his new school and is happy to have his own room again.

Simon continues to struggle with his eating disorder and is still eating a small diet but has stopped running. He has stopped his weighing ritual and is a little more relaxed about his weight. He still has anxiety and bad days but, on the whole, has more good days than bad. The new start seems to have served us well, and Simon and I are getting along fine.

Daniel is finishing school in 2019, but as he has a National Disability Insurance Scheme plan, I feel confident that I will be able to find him a suitable program. Seeing everyone so happy, it is easy to believe that things are going to be OK for us, maybe even good. For the first time since Daniel's diagnosis, I feel able to cope, and I have hope for the future. It is a great feeling, and I love it.

About the Author

Elizabeth lives in Queensland and is a happily married mother to two teenagers. This is her first book.

www.ingramcontent.com/pod-product-compliance
Lightning Source LLC
Chambersburg PA
CBHW030910080526
44589CB00010B/233